You By You

--

How to connect YOU
to younger self?

--

Vikram:

ISBN: 9798888833001
First Edition: 2021
Second Edition: 2022

Dedicated to my
true younger self
my son
Viyaan

You By You

Vikrmn:

ACKNOWLEDGMENTS

I am thankful to Ekta
who supported me and also took care of
me and our *true younger self*
while I was busy writing this one.

1.

Echo

The speed of love is measured in...

◈

The speed of love
is measured in
blushes per hour.

--

"Time travel is real," said the lady. She was in her sixties but still curious as ever; never cured of the traveller's spirit that had brought her to this spot once more.

"True that," said the old man walking next to her, his hand in hers. He smiled. His gaze never left her face. "Decades together, and it's the ice age again – that's nothing short of a time travel marvel."

She exhaled and smiled at the frosty cloud of breath that came with it. "Indeed. It's three degrees here. For me, it's an ice age."

It was difficult to walk with their heavy winter gear and trainers. But she loved talking up any challenge with him by her side. As they walked past a moistened glass door, they caught a rather funny-looking reflection. The couple stopped and childishly held their hands together to form the shape of a heart. They looked at each other and laughed heartily as they stole the moment.

By the time they reached the Queen's Palace in Windsor, the man was out of breath. "Do we have to cover Buckingham Palace on this trip?"

"Yes!" She laughed as she pointed to a bench nearby. "You have never taken me to Buckingham Palace even once since we moved here."

"I am hell tired," he grumbled as he trudged towards the bench.

"I guess the old wisdom that *'humans sweat less as they age'* is nothing but a myth. Just look at you!"

He wheezed as he leaned forward and sat. "Quite right, I am sweating buckets. Is it still wisdom if it's contrary to life?"

He pulled off his cap and fanned himself. They both sat for a while as they looked at the tourists passing by.

Suddenly, a loud noise startled her, and she jerked forward.

"YOU!" She fumed as she clutched her chest. "Why do you change the notification tone very often? It'll give us a mini heart attack someday!"

"Ah!" He chuckled as he pulled out his mobile phone. "But nothing has happened to me so far."

As he was about to unlock his phone, a palace guard approached him. "Sir, no photography allowed."

"My apologies," he said and put the phone back in his pocket.

"Thank you," she smirked. "You better not spoil this trip with your camera pointed at your face."

"It was an e-mail notification. I wasn't going to take any photo."

"Oh, whatever."

After a brief rest, the couple continued with their trip. They explored the castle and made more sweet memories. They clicked selfies with pouts. They also left some of the other tourists in splits when they asked them to click their salsa poses.

Later that evening, after the castle trip, they returned to the city. Seated at a restaurant, she was lost in her reveries, reminiscing over the view of the London Bridge.

"Does that remind you of something?" She quipped.

He followed her gaze and grinned ear to ear as if he could read the memories etched in her mind.

"Of course I remember," he replied and pulled out his phone. "I do remember that I got a notification, and as soon as I pulled out my phone, the guard came and stopped the greatest photographer of the century from taking a photo of the decade! Except that he wasn't even taking any."

"You are such a killjoy," she fumed. "Do you remember the first time we visited it?"

"Be specific," he teased her.

"Nothing." She scrolled down the menu as she hummed a tune to avoid a conversation.

"The speed of love is measured in blushes per hour." He said in a teasing low voice, with his nose still buried in his cell phone.

She blushed crimson, despite her best efforts to keep her expression neutral.

The man continued, "Oh, and you were looking drop-dead gorgeous in that lovely red gown."

"Awwwww, you remember!"

"No," he replied, looking at his phone, "I just pulled up the geo-location history of that place on my phone. Hence I remember."

"Very, very funny," she said and started reading the menu.

After what seemed like an eternal silence, she asked, "What happened? Which geo-tag did you wander off to?"

He showed her the mobile screen and said, "Have a look at this e-mail."

She shot a casual glance at the screen and asked, "Yeah, so?"

"Check the date."

Adjusting her glasses, she took a closer look. "Really, fifteen years hence?"

The man nodded with a smile.

"A mail from the future?"

The man could only nod as he was short of words.

"YOU! Oh my God!" She jumped out of her seat, sat on his lap, and smothered him with kisses. "You cracked it. YOU! You did it, honey!"

She was too overjoyed to care about the people around them. People were fascinated with the old couple's display of affection. They had no idea what they were talking about.

"Oh, wow," she pointed outside. "Look."

He looked at the tiny snowflakes as they floated down the sky. He was over excited, felt his left eye flicker and his jaw twitch as emotions swept over his face. He looked up at the sky and closed his eyes. His emotions made his voice tremble. "We did it for you. I wish you were here. We did it for you."

"Yes," she cheered. "We did it for her. Let's drink to the honour of the Great Woman. The great lady who…."

His ringing phone cut her short. She grabbed the phone from him as soon as she saw the caller ID. "We have the best news!" She screamed in excitement.

Unable to contain her excitement, she rose to her feet and chatted animatedly. Unaware, she started to walk away from him. The person on the other side began to speak. Her excitement slowly faded as she tried to make sense of what the other person spoke.

The voice from the other end, packed with panic, screamed, "Don't let him read the e-mail. I repeat. DO NOT let him read it."

She was still confused. She instinctively turned to look at him. He was lying flat on the ground, his face up. He was unconscious! The damage was done.

Her heart raced, and her eyes moistened. The mobile slipped from her hand. She rushed towards him. She bent down and shook him. "Get up, are you alright? Please respond". There was no response.

People rushed to help her as she sat there and sobbed. Her body trembled as she panicked. She tried to calm herself down but in vain.

The faint voice from her mobile still echoed…

"Don't tell him right now. He won't be able to bear the news. I repeat… DO NOT…"

**

2.

Oblivious

Life is like a painting...

◈

Life is like a painting;
make yours a masterpiece.

--

<>

~ 50 years back~

<>

"Two flat whites, please," said the man, in his 60s. He then turned to face the girl next to him and asked, "Nia. Sugar?"

The girl, lost in her reveries, did not hear him. He followed her gaze to a poster that he couldn't read.

He gently jolted her out of her daydream.

"Oh! Sorry?"

"Sugar?"

"Yup, two please, brown."

As they walked out, the man looked at the poster the girl had been gawking at. It had green and red bell peppers printed all over it. The word "Contest" was printed out in bold.

"Miss dreamer!" He smiled, taking a quick sip. "Sorry,

sir, just daydreaming."

"Doesn't matter if you can dream it or not. All that matters is if you can begin it or not. Take that first step." He said as he stepped down the stairs. She stood there, a little lost.

"You know, even I was..."

Before he could complete the sentence, someone shoved him. He spilled the coffee all over himself. Even her dress had coffee stains.

"Who the hell!" He yelled and turned to see who had shoved him.

A boy in his twenties was trying to rush past him, but in a hurry, he ended up bumping into him.

He glared at the boy, who looked pale with fright. The boy seemed familiar, but he couldn't seem to place him.

The boy started apologizing fervently. The man suddenly remembered. "Youvik?"

The boy looked at the man's face clearly for the first time.

"Mr. Singh?" Youvik was smiling and confused at the same time.

Oblivious to the conversation, the girl was busy wiping the coffee stains on her dress with a tissue.

"Hey, Youvik." Mr. Singh waved at him, "How are you?"

"I'm good, sir. Thanks. Good to see you," he replied, though seemed eager to end the conversation.

Mr. Singh sensed his impatience, "All's well?"

"Yes, sir, but right now, I'm in a hurry." He said and walked backwards, "Sir, I will catch up with you some other time."

"Careful, there's..." but before Mr. Singh could complete his sentence, Youvik banged his head on the pole.

He stopped for a minute, rubbed his head, and disappeared into thin air.

Mr. Singh smiled and said to the girl, "It's Youvik, you know."

"Stupid fellow! He ruined my new dress," she said as she struggled to wipe off the stains.

"Rinse it with salt and baking soda."

"Oh, how? Does it work?"

"Leave it. Give it to your mom. Mothers know everything." He chuckled, "I'll go and grab another coffee."

By the moment he came back, Nia was still looking at the poster.

"You still lost?"

"Hmm," she nodded, "I sort of liked it, looks freshly painted, so lively."

"Agree."

"I wish I count make my life that lively."

"Life is like a painting; make yours a masterpiece." Quoted Mr. Singh.

"Actually, true."

"So tell me, what's troubling you? Where are you lost?"

She thought for a while and replied, "I don't know how to put it in words, sir."

They walked towards the zebra crossing nearby. They chatted non-stop as they slowly sipped their coffees till they finished it.

"People may create your dreams with you, but not for you. It's you and only you who has to think, start and continue," said Mr. Singh as they walked along.

Youvik, meanwhile, had managed to get on the bus and leave the station.

**

3.

Zeal

Perfection is the pure action...

◈

Perfection is the pure action
that comes with the zeal to excel.

--

Somewhere in Chandigarh, a man in his mid-fifties, was busy sorting a few documents.

The sizzling noise of *Tadka* (tempering) and an aromatic flavour drew him to the kitchen. He couldn't resist himself as he walked into the kitchen with the documents.

"Riya Madam! Is it our anniversary today?" He asked, peeping into the kitchen.

The lady busy chopping tomatoes, looked up and said, "No Verma *Ji,* it was yesterday."

"Was it?" He tried to recall the date. "No, no, you are joking."

"Well, who started it?"

"I just asked as something delectable is being cooked."

"Mr. Neel! Are you trying to say that I cook well only on our anniversary?"

"No, ma'am, not at all. You cook amazing dishes every day. That was a compliment for *the beautiful* aroma filling the house." He pulled her closer to him. "Same as you."

She dragged the chopping board between them and said, "Can you please chop some coriander."

"Oh, God," The man frowned and looked at the documents. "I have lots of work. But I will surely do it after I file this policy document."

"Good," she snapped at him as she picked up the ladle, "So choose policy or coriander."

"Don't ruin the mood by calling it coriander baby," he moved closer to her. "It's cilantro."

At that very moment, the doorbell rang.

"Go now," she smirked and chimed aloud, "Coming!"

The doorbell rang repeatedly.

"Coming, coming." She ran towards the door with the ladle in her hand.

She opened the door and waved the ladle. "YOU? Can't you wait?" She asked, visibly annoyed.

The bump on his head immediately caught her attention. "Oh, God. What happened, *Puttar* (kiddo)?"

"Dude," he said as he entered the house. "I am alright. I was in a hurry."

"Is everything alright? You're home early from college today. By the way, where is Tinku?" She peeked out.

"He is still at college," he replied.

"I left without informing him."He said quickly and rushed to his study room.

"YOU!" She followed him, "Youvik! Tell me the truth. What happened?"

"I was doing brown sugar when the police raid happened. If they come asking for me, tell them I left for London."

She hit him with the ladle, softly.

"Ouch." He rubbed his shoulder and bent down to plug in the CPU power cable. "We went to the cyber cafe, but there was a long queue outside. I had to reply to a few urgent emails, so I came back."

"Are you sure?"

"What's wrong with you, Ma?" He looked at her and said with a sincere expression, "Trust me, everything's fine."

"*Kha meri kasam* (Swear on me)."

"*Kasam;* national food of this country. *Kasam ki jagah khana khilado* (Offer me some food instead of vows)."

She sat next to him and remarked, "You are trying to switch on the computer without even turning on the UPS, and you are asking me not to worry."

"Uh-uh." He plugged in the UPS and entered the password.

"Trust me. Everything is okay."

"Okay," she got up and went to the kitchen. "I trust you."

He entered the login password and a dialogue box popped up. "Incorrect Password."

"Dude," he irritably called out to her. "What's the password?"

"Ask Daddy," she retorted.

"He must be busy star gazing. You tell me."

"Ask daddy."

"No, you tell me. I saw you video-calling *Maasi* last night. So you must be knowing the password. And why does Dad have to change the password every month?"

"Ask Daddy," she repeated.

"No, I won't ask daddy, you tell me," he went to the kitchen. He touched the nasty bump on his head and asked, "How can a mother see her own son in pain and still torture him?"

"*Nautanki* (Drama)."

"If you tell me the password, I'll tell you who I ran into today, after two years."

"Ask daddy!" She screamed.

"I am not having lunch till..."

Before he got a chance to complete the sentence, she roared. "Ask Daddy. ALL CAPS."

"Oh, I see. Dad is witty but not this password."

"How did you know that it's without any space," she laughed.

"Smart people, you know," he said as he took a bite off a tomato.

"By the way, my smart 'people,' I set this password, not Daddy, and the new rule is that no one will change this password ever." She patted him on his head.

"Ouch," he rubbed his head and walked back to the study room.

She heated the tea towel on the cook-top and followed him. She gently rubbed the bump on his head with a hot cloth and said, "*Perfection is the pure action that comes with the zeal to excel.*"

"Oh! Mr. Singh! Your English teacher?"

Youvik nodded.

"He used to repeat that phrase quite often. When did he come back from London?"

He shrugged. "No idea."

"He is a true gentleman. He always treated me like his younger sister, and you like a nephew," she went back to the kitchen. "Do you recall who advised you to pursue a career in Information Technology?"

"I know, Ma," he nodded as he absent-mindedly ransacked the mailbox. "It was him."

As Riya got busy with the kitchen work, Youvik keenly scrolled through his mailbox. Then he jumped to the Recycle folder and skimmed through the deleted e-mails. After finding nothing relevant, he slid back on the chair and shouted out of the blue. "Oh, God."

"Why are you disturbing God? Tell me," she shouted from the kitchen.

"I can't believe that I deleted the e-mails," he bellowed, thumping the table.

"Oh! That small thing? Refer it to God, please."

"Thanks, it helped."

"Check your backup, just in case," she prompted.

"Dude! Where do you get these ideas from?" He rushed to the e-mail settings. "I am jealous of your zeal."

**

4.

Loop

Mysteries, like black and white...

◈

Mysteries, like black and white,
the salt and pepper of colours;
for life tastes bland without them.

--

"I am hungry. Is lunch ready?" Neel asked as he walked towards the dining table.

"You bought this t-shirt and Bermuda last week only," she remarked and began to arrange the food on the table. "Why are you wearing it at home?"

Neel jingled. "Black and white color, as if lovers are made for each other."

"Not again please," she sighed, "Please help me arrange the table once in a while."

"Love you too, baby," he laughed as he pulled out some plates from the cupboard.

"Dad! Again with the black and white outfit?" Youvik quipped as he joined them and filled the water bottles. "Why do you love black and white so much?"

"Because..."

Neel was about to reply, but she interrupted him, "Are you fine, Yuvi?"

"Yes. Why?"

"Do you need anything?"

"No."

"Money for a trip or gadgets?" She quipped.

"Nah, why?" Youvik replied, confused.

"Or do you want me to meet your girlfriend?"

"Sorry?" He looked at his father.

"Why would he ask you to meet his girlfriendsssss?" Neel giggled.

"Dad!"

She smirked, "Any Indian mother would get worried if her son starts helping out at home. Like filling water bottles and putting them in the fridge. Like what you just did".

"Ah, this?" He realized he had never done it before, "Oh, it's just like that."

"Mommy is not used to this big happiness my boy," she said as she caressed his chin.

"*Kuch bhi* (Illogical)!" He opened the fridge door and asked, "Anyways! Do you believe in time travel?"

She was serving the salad when she froze after hearing his question. She looked at Neel with shock.

He looked back at her. It looked as though they were hiding something.

"*Puttar,* mysteries are like the black and white color."

"Sorry?" Youvik was clueless.

"Mysteries like black and white are the salt and pepper of colours. Life tastes bland without them." Neel narrated with a smile and pointed at the salt and pepper shakers, "Could you pass them, please?"

Youvik noticed that his mother was lost in her own thoughts.

"Ma?"

"Yup, sorry."

"Can you please pass on Salt," asked Neel. Youvik asked at the same time, "Do you believe in time travel?"

"No," replied Riya but her tone had changed drastically.

"Why," they both asked together and then looked at each other.

Mother looked at both of them and replied, "It's not possible."

"Why?" They again chimed in chorus and then looked at each other.

She passed the shakers to Neel, walked to Youvik, took the bottles from him and stacked them in the refrigerator one by one.

"What about my why?" Youvik pulled a chair.

She took out curd container from refrigerator and came back to the table.

"See, the logic is simple," she demonstrated by pouring spoonfuls of curd into a bowl rather quickly. "To travel fast, you need to increase the speed. So it is possible to travel to the future with a time machine without defying the laws of string theory, but..."

"But what?" He looked at the curd bowl eagerly.

"But to go back in time, you cannot rely on moving. Not only faster speed but also slow speed will fail to help you."

"Then? What's the solution?"

"You need something called a negative speed," she

said firmly.

"I am confused," said Youvik as he sat down and picked up the bowl to serve food.

"Let me explain," She continued, "To boil water, you need to heat it to at least a hundred degrees. To freeze it, you need to do the opposite with negative temperature."

"Right," Youvik nodded in agreement.

"So, to go further ahead in time, you need a rising high speed, and to go to the past, you would need?"

"A negative speed?" Youvik was awestruck. He never reckoned his mother could explain something as complicated as time travel with such ease.

"Does the analogy fit?"

Youvik nodded, mesmerized, "Dude! You are a genius."

"So for time travel, you would need a speedometer that shows negative speed."

"Ma, you should write a white paper on time travel."

"Hah! Gone are the days when I used to do all that. It's been thirty years since I completed my masters."

Neel added, "She indeed wrote a white paper on time travel for her Ph.D. But no one cared enough to publish it."

She sighed, "So I gave up."

Youvik got up and embraced her warmly.

"And this hug was for?"

"I know you did it for us," he smiled.

"I am in no mood to cry," she patted him on the shoulder as tears rolled down his cheeks.

"Aww, my baby," she caressed his head, "I have made your favourite dish."

"Hmm."

"Pizza with..."

Youvik instantly groaned, "Nooo."

"Yes!"

"My favourite dish is *Rajmah chawal* (kidney beans with rice), not pizza with boiled *Rajmah* toppings."

And yet, as they ate the pizza, Youvik couldn't stop licking his fingers. Riya looked at him mockingly, with her eyebrows arched.

"I don't like it in general, but it is a little tasty today," he shrugged.

"You know," she continued seriously. "Something called mail-loop is actually possible."

Youvik was eating the pizza with such dedication that he didn't fully pay attention to what she had just said. "Yeah, whatever, but for now, I am happy-high on this pizza."

"Dad," he said, licking his fingers. "By the way, why did you buy a t-shirt with pink text on it?"

"Is it pink?" He looked down at his t-shirt. "I thought it was grey."

She looked at him and asked, "You forgot? You bought it to please me."

"Oh, yeah, I remember."

"I can never understand you both," Youvik commented as he continued biting into the Pizza.

<>

Gazing at the sunset from his rooftop, Youvik

furrowed his eyebrows. He was glaring at the distance with his worried eyes.

"*Bro*, here, have this. You really need to relax."

"No, Tinku," Youvik mumbled, took the teacup from him, "It's weird and somewhat serious."

"Does someone have your private photos or something?" Tinku winked.

"Someone is impersonating me," Youvik said in a worried tone. He got up. "And look at you... cracking jokes?"

"Chill! Take it lightly, man, sit down, and take a sip." Tinku reassured him. He tugged his arm and said with a smile, "I made it especially for you."

Shaking his head, Youvik sat down and took a sip. Even before he swallowed it, he knew what it was. He looked at the teacup and then at Tinku.

Tinku smiled and beamed with pride. "I added two shots from my Dad's exquisite collection of heavenly spirits!"

Youvik's smile faded, "I am distraught. Someone is trying to impersonate me by hacking my email."

"Loosen up, bro."Tinku patted him, "Tell me, what's the point of impersonation if someone is using your mail to send the stuff to you only?"

"Point; but how would I know?"

"Okay, tell me, who was the sender?"

"Someone sent the emails from my own email ID."

"What was there in the mails?"

"It just said, 'Test 1'."

"Subject?" Tinku was surprised.

"Yes. Test 1."

"That's it?"

"Yes."

"I don't see any issue here," Tinku shrugged.

"I received not one, but six mails back to back. So I ran back home worried that someone is trying to hack my social media accounts."

"Oh, I see," said Tinku, slurped his tea and thought for a while.

"What about all the dirty messages you subscribed to, from your e-mail account?" He wiggled his eyebrows. "Don't you think one of them hacked your mailbox and posted about your subscriptions on social media?"

"This is why I did not want to discuss it with you in the first place."

"*Chameli* (Sweety)," Tinku pulled his cheek and said, "Forward the mail to me. I'll get it checked by some IT pro."

"I cannot find that mail anywhere!"

"Did you look in the Archive or Spam folder?"

"It's not in Archive. I'll check in the Spam folder."

"You know, when my girlfriend dumped me..."

"Not this again, please."

Tinku continued unabated, "*We were both there yet alone. 'Bye,' she said and left, and I was all alone again.*"

"Was this your third break-up or fourth?"

"Sixth." Tinku was in a retrospective mood, "I got to know that she already had a boyfriend in stand-by mode."

"Sorry?" Remarked Youvik, clearly startled.

"Back-up, boyfriend."

"Have you lost it?"

Tinku smiled, "Back-up, my friend, backup."

"Ohhh!" Youvik rolled his eyes.

Tinku smirked, "In job, money and files, ensure you have back-up, before you discard."

Youvik sighed and gulped down the last sip of his 'tea.'

"One second." Tinku's eyes twinkled; he remembered something.

"You wrote me an email when I had created my new mail ID. I remember that it had read 'Test 1' in the subject line and mail body."

"Yeah, so?"

"Probably you would have registered on some website that sends you scheduled emails."

Youvik thought about it for a minute and shook his head in disagreement. "Even then, how can they send me a mail from my own ID?"

"Take a sip and try to remember."

Youvik looked at his empty cup.

"Back-cup," said Tinku. He extended his hand to give Youvik his cup. "Backup."

Youvik took a sip, gave the cup back, and closed his eyes for a while. Tinku stared at him with the hope that he would remember something.

"Argh, I cannot remember doing any such thing, Tinku," Youvik said. He grew restless with each passing second.

"Hmm," Tinku scratched his chin, "Then someone is sending you e-mails from the future for sure."

"Of course," Youvik smirked, "Because this is a sci-fi

movie, and I am the hero."

"Haha! Anyway, what are your weekend plans? How about a movie night?" Tinku tried to divert his attention.

"No plans. I have to study."

"By the way, Monica will be joining us."

"Um, I'll try to squeeze out some time." Youvik smiled sheepishly.

Tinku was about to say something when they heard a knock on the door.

"Shh. It must be my mom. Please don't tell her about the tea."

Tinku's mother opened the door and smiled at them.

"Hello, aunty," Youvik greeted. He struggled hard not to laugh.

"Hello Yuvi," she replied with a smile. Seeing the tea cup in Tinku's hand, she moved forward to take it from him.

Youvik immediately took the cup from Tinku's hand, finished the remaining tea in a single gulp, and smiled at her. "Thanks for the tasty tea, aunty."

She moved on to dry the clothes. "Can you please ask Tinku to improve his grades?" She said with a smile, "He has become so lousy these days. All he does is drink tea and talk to God only knows who all day."

"I talk to Youvik all day, Ma," Tinku prompted.

"What is this Tinku?" Youvik added, mockingly, "You should study hard. Let me take you for a motivational movie this weekend so that you can get inspiration and concentrate on your studies."

"Good," his mother nodded in approval.

"A movie is a mirror to life; you live experiences without going through." Tinku added.

"Yes," Youvik chirped in, "Aunty, don't worry. I'll take care of it."

"Thank you, son." She patted him on his head.

<>

Later that evening, Youvik, back home, savaged his mailbox.

"I will figure this out," he said on the phone, "Mysteries are meant to be solved. Anyway, you carry on, Tinku. Bye."

As he hung up, he scrolled through the spam section. He found a mail that read 'Test 1'. "Finally," he sighed.

Upon opening the mail, he noticed that the sender and recipient's addresses were the same.

"Scheduled mail?" He said, thinking out loud, "Which website did I register at?"

"YOU," Riya shouted at the top of her lungs, "Dinner is ready. Ask daddy if he is done with his stargazing."

He shut down the computer and went upstairs, yelling, "Dad! Daaaaaad!"

"Yes," his father smiled as he stepped down the stairs, *"Roof-tops catch-ups are awesome, be it dinners, be it stargazing; with loved ones."*

"Your loved one is in the kitchen."

"Amm, I was talking about my telescope and stars."

"Okay, then it's fine," Youvik teased as he followed him.

"So what new star did you find today?"

"Not new, but an old fact that every star in the sky is bigger and brighter than the sun; different color."

"Which color?"

"Like black and white." Neel was all smiles as they entered the living room. *"Black and white as if phoenix of colours has eloped into opacity."*

"Not again," Youvik exclaimed.

"Ok fine, tell me how many planets are there?"

"Eight planets have been confirmed, and the ninth one is yet to be confirmed."

"Right, but our Indian mythological system already declared that there are nine so many centuries ago."

"Yeah, I know."

"But considering the pace of global warming, it looks as though mankind will lose one for sure."

"Yeah, I know."

"Kids in the future will look at photos of this beautiful, centuries-old planet and ask..." Neel chuckled, *"Wow! So beautiful. Which star was this? It was a Planet, not a star, it WAS called Earth."*

"Seems to me like a dialogue from a sci-fi movie."

<>

Youvik was on his bed, his eyes drooped shut.

"*Mysteries…*" he murmured, recalling his father's words and the mail he received from his own ID.

**

5.

Purpose

Life, if you please...

◈

Life, if you please;
bundle of surprises,
it is.

--

It was just like any other day for his family. Youvik was busy with his studies. Riya was sipping tea on the rooftop, drying her hair, and basking in the evening sun. But her focus was on her old thesis papers. She was going through it seriously and was circling a few words here and there.

At that moment, the doorbell rang. "YOU," she shouted, an indication for Youvik to open the door.

"I am studying," Youvik shouted back as he scrolled through his computer screen. "Daaaaad!"

Neel shook his head and got up, "Everyone is busy these days. I think I am the only unemployed person in this house."

He opened the door and was surprised to see two of his old friends.

"We were just passing by, so we thought we'd say hi," one of them explained. Neel greeted them with a warm hug.

"YOU," he shouted, asking Youvik to come down to meet his friends.

They sat down to chat, and Youvik served them with a cold drink.

"YOU?" Asked a friend, pointing at Neel. "What is that?"

"Not what, it's a who," Neel smiled, "YOU, is for Youvik."

They looked at Youvik, and he smiled back, greeted them, made small talk, and then went straight to his room.

"*Bhabhi Ji*? (Sister-in-law?)" Asked one of his friends.

"Upstairs," he replied. "She'll join us."

They continued chatting. After some time, Neel got up and said, "I'll be back with some snacks."

"We are good," they said, but he insisted.

"Okay, but with coffee, please," said one of his friends with a wink.

"Ah! The Kitchen King," one of them teased him. "I remember you liked playing with kitchen sets, too."

A fit of laughter broke out.

Neel came into the living room, whisking the coffee, "If WOMEN can handle office work and kitchen chores together, WE-MEN too, can try to do the same?"

"Well, your choice. You can. We won't." One friend winked at the other.

Another friend said, in a low voice to the other, "Some men think, not the cigarette butt, but working in the kitchen reduces their 'importance'."

Both of them laughed heartily.

"Ahem!" Neel shushed him as soon as he noticed Riya

enter the living room. He said loudly, *"Black and white is the mix of toughest simplicity and easiest complexity."*

Another friend promptly understood and commented, "So intellectual."

Riya greeted them and laid out some biscuits for the guests.

"Did he start with his black and white intellectual thingy again?"

"Namaste, Bhabhi Ji." The friends greeted her.

The first friend took the mug and whisker from Neel's hands and said, "I want to learn the art of coffee whisking to impress my wife. It will be much better than the 'black and white tea.'"

"Namaste bhai saab (brother). Making coffee is not rocket science. Make a cup of coffee for your wife and she'll teach you if it turns out bad," she chuckled.

They all laughed and settled down.

"Bhabhi Ji! How is your online coaching going on?" One of the friends asked.

"So far, so good," she replied. Asking for the mug and whisker from him, she said as she went to kitchen, "You guys talk, I'll do it."

"I can do it if you want," Neel said, sat on the sofa, stretched his legs, and yawned. *"Love is like coffee; the better you brew it, the lovelier it ages."*

"Dad," Youvik screamed from his room. "All talk, no show."

"Gotcha." Riya shouted from the kitchen.

Neel and his friends continued to talk for a while.

"So, what's the plan for *Dushehra*?" Neel asked them.

“I am planning to kill our boss,” One of the friends’ replied.

“Ram-fication of Ravan-ous thoughts is what Dushehra is all about.” Replied the other.

“Prabhu (Almighty),” Neel and the other friend bowed to him together.

Youvik and Riya could hear their bouts of laughter.

<>

Making his bed, Youvik realized that he could not stop thinking about it.

His phone chimed. It was mail. It read ‘The Purpose.’

He ignored it – "must be some online course." He was about to keep his phone down when he noticed the sender. This mail, too, was sent from his own e-mail id.

His heart pounded as he opened the mail and read it…

<>

Dear YOU,

I hope life is kind to you. I hope you are going on the right track.

“Hope you are living your dreams or dreaming of living with hope.”

Mom is going to Guru Ji’s ashram. A saint is visiting.

More than a saint, he is a philosopher and a scholar. The above quote is from one of his speeches. Try to take out some time and join your mother.

Yours truly,
YOU

<>

He ran to the kitchen, "Ma! You were telling me about some *Ashram*?"

"Yes."

"But why through a mail?"

"Sorry?" She was confused. "I was about to tell you about it, but I was not sure of the timing."

"Oh. Is it?"

"Yes. And what mail are you talking about?"

Youvik paused for a moment, "Are you sure you didn't send me a mail?"

"I'm sure, but what's the matter?"

He thought for a while and replied, "Nothing."

"Anyway, who is taking me to *Guru Ji's Ashram*?"

"Dude," Youvik prompted, "Ask Daddy. You know that I hate anything related to religion."

"*Guru Ji* once said," she said, looking at Neel, "*One religion, one civilization, above all is Love and Humanity, respectively.*"

Neel smiled as he knew he had no other option and nodded, "I'll drop you."

<>

"Life, if you please; bundle of surprises, it is." The saint remarked. He had a radiant glow on his face, despite being in his mid-70s.

"But sometimes, life goes on and on, and you find happiness in that bundle. You are no longer curious about what life brings you as a bundle of surprises. You just patiently go with the flow of life,"

"Journey leading to just an end is better lost on the way. Who knows, you would explore the real destination." He added.

Riya, sitting among the audience in the saint's Ashram, smiled and nodded. She looked over her left and noticed Youvik looking around, uninterested in the event.

"You," the saint pointed at all in the audience, "Sometimes, you are baffled by impatience. Life repeats itself aimlessly."

The moment the saint said YOU, Youvik turned attentive. It was as though the saint was there only for his enlightenment. He now seemed a little interested in the saint's words.

"You," the saint added, "Are born for a purpose, and I can prove it."

"Just think about any famous invention or product, and the name of its inventor comes to your mind. Electricity, bulb, smart phone, electric car, operating system etc. all of them were invented by someone. Each invention was the purpose of someone's life."

"If they wouldn't have invented it, someone else from

their generation or the next generation would have done so."

"Your life has a purpose, and if not, give it one."

"At times," the saint continued, "You find yourself on a mysterious track where you are unaware of your goals. You keep wondering how to give direction to the aimlessness, to the storm of thoughts in your mind. But this impatience is essential in making you the real *YOU*. If you keep living in a happy bubble, it will soon burst and reveal how shallow and ignorant you have been."

Every time the saint said YOU, Youvik seemed to be going in a trance. It appeared to him that the saint was there, speaking only for him. He realized that he was there for a purpose.

<>

On their way back home, Youvik drove the scooter with Riya in the rear seat. He kept mum, thinking something. The words of the saint were still resonating in his ears…

"Everyone is different. So it is essential to explore yourself to understand your mind. Short goals are those which you can achieve in a matter of months. The long ones are those for which you toil your entire life. I hope you find some clarity about these soon. I hope you unearth the essential things in life from layers of pettiness and ignorance that may have set in."

<>

"You," Riya tapped his shoulders. "Stop the scooter at the next junction. I have to buy medicines."

They went in at the chemist, and as they came out, she stopped. Youvik looked at her and followed her gaze. She was looking at the *Golgappa* (water-balls) vendor.

"You are on medication. You know that?" He asked.

"You know, when you were a kid..." she said with a smile.

"Yeah, I know," he mimicked her. "My teeth were rotten, but you still used to give me one chocolate toffee without telling Dad."

"I'll have just one." She requested.

The next moment, she was enjoying *Golgappas* back-to-back.

"You said just one," Youvik looked at her, "These give you a hit more than tequila shots, right?"

She extended her plate towards Youvik. He leaned back, holding the scooter as he guzzled the *Golgappa* down in one shot.

"More?"

"You know that I hate *Golgappas,*" he replied and went back to his mobile to read more about the saint.

"You are known by the thoughts you seed." Read the quote on a website.

"Once you start your professional career, the goals will change inevitably. In fact, when the long-term goal sets in, short-term aspirations seep in and continuously replace them.

For example, a short-term goal to set up an alternative source of income or to enhance your technical qualification, or bodybuilding while doing a job, or preparation for a tournament, and so many more."

"These are transient. Even if you subtract one or two from these, life won't become a disaster. Don't get too upset when things don't go as planned."

<>

"Done," said Riya as she paid the *Golgappa wala* and sat on the scooter.

The guy ran to them with some money, "Aunty *Ji*!"

"Keep the change," she smiled, "Buy some chocolates for your kids."

Youvik looked at her and smiled. He kick-started the scooter, and said, "Seems like you are either influenced a little extra by *Guru Ji*..."

"Or?"

"Or you are a little happy-high on *Golgappas*."

"Very *phunny*."

As they headed back home, she asked, "All good?"

"Why?"

"You are driving so calm," she chuckled, "Not yelling at other people on the road."

The thought of the unknown emails circled back to his mind, and he smiled, "Yup, now all is good."

He was not scared of the e-mails any more.

<>

At night, Youvik was thinking about the saint. He found an online video of the saint and played it.

"Life is like a painting. Imagine it, and try drawing it with a pencil first, then fill in the colours of happiness, correct the mistakes with the eraser of love and forgiveness; hence, one dream project is accomplished. Create more masterpieces just like that."

"So short-term goals might come and go, but what is the purpose of life? Could you give it a serious thought? To help yourself find the purpose of life, make a list of things you like and hobbies that you enjoy pursuing.

Give your best while studying. This long-term goal will define your life and the footprints you leave behind for others to follow. So.."

He played all videos back to back until he reached the last one.

"Defeat none but one; yourself; for a better self than you were before."

While watching the videos, he convinced himself that this too was like one of those silly motivational videos he had clicked on mindlessly in the past.

And that was why he was getting bombarded with spam messages.

<>

"Light is still on," Neel said as he came into the room

and found Youvik asleep. He took off the headphone from Youvik's ears and pulled the bed sheet over him.

<>

"It was a wonderful session," said Youvik, "I saw your mom but not you."

He sat across the visibly shy Monica. They were both feeling shy to talk to each other.

"Yeah, I was at home," she smiled, "Had some work to do."

"The Saint was really good."

"Are we here to talk about him or us?" She asked teasingly.

Youvik smiled, "We just saw a movie together. It was our first date. It will take me time to open up."

"Tell me something nice about me," she leaned towards him.

"Hey, I think I have seen you somewhere."

She was surprised.

"Oh," Youvik said as he snapped his finger, "I know you; you are the girl I always see in my dreams."

"Aww," she blushed, "That's so cute. I didn't know you were so romantic."

<>

"Cover your head," Riya instructed Youvik, and she quickly shared her *Dupatta* (stole) on his head.

"Does it matter to God?" Youvik asked.

"Peace bestows, be it spiritual, be it religious; with faith."

The family was preparing for *Diwali Poojan*. Neel had arranged a plate full of fruits and other sweets as an offering for Goddess Lakshmi and Lord Ganesha, while Riya had lit incense sticks and *diya* for the *Aarti*.

Later in the evening, relatives and friends visited them with gifts and sweets. Youvik wasn't too pleased to have so many people around.

"Sometimes I feel we Indians celebrate too many festivals," Youvik said as they were having dinner.

"True." Neel nodded in agreement. "*Throughout the year, in all religions, in all seasons; we Indians find reasons, to worship almost everything and everyone; from people to Gods; from animals to plants; from planets to stars. So our spirits are always high with small surprises of life, we cherish meeting and greeting people, for we celebrate every aspect of being human.*"

"That is all we do," she added with a pious smile. "*Not just the festivals, but it's about the people you celebrate with.*"

"*Maate* (Ma), I wish you had invented some *Samay Yatra Yantra* (Time Travel Machine)," Youvik ribbed as he raised a toast. "I would go back and not ask this question."

"*Nautanki* (Drama)," she laughed.

"But that's a good one, I'll post it to my status today," he jumped to grab his phone.

"With a little modification," she added.

"Sure, go on."

"Throughout the year, in all regions, in all seasons; we HINDUS find reasons, to worship almost anything and everything, anyone and everyone; from people to Gods;

from animals to plants; from planets to stars. So our spirits are always high with small surprises of life, we cherish meeting and greeting people, for in SANATAN DHARMA we celebrate every aspect of being human. We believe Bhagwan (God) is in every single particle and OM is in every single ATOM of the universe."

"Awesome," he smiled and posted, "Credits: My mommy."

**

6.

Monotony

Beware of will power...

◈

Beware of will power.
It damages your giving-up skills.

--

<>

3 years later

<>

Youvik slumped against the sofa as soon as he came home.

"Ma, I need coffee," he muttered, his voice barely audible.

"How was the interview?" Riya asked as he dunked a biscuit in his cup.

"Not good," he said with a sigh. "They asked for experience, and I don't have any."

"Hmm," she said with a nod. "Ask them how you'll get experience without getting your first job."

"I actually did," Youvik smiled.

"Seriously??"

"Yup, but they said it's the criteria."

"Don't worry, keep trying."

"Yeah, I am, but.," Youvik replied. The biscuit broke, and a part of it fell into the teacup unnoticed.

"But?" Neel joined them for snacks.

Youvik plastered on a tight smile.

"Good evening," he said as he sat near him, "But what?"

"Hmm," Youvik continued, "But I am sort of tired now."

"What candles are to cake; joy is to happiness; and happiness, to life." she consoled him.

"Maate," he bowed to her.

"Do you know what the term averaging-out means?" Neel asked..

"Nope."

"It's a share market term. You buy some more of loss-making shares to bring down the average cost."

Youvik was still silent.

Neel dipped the biscuit in his cup, and said seriously, "Sometimes you have to risk another biscuit to save the lost one."

"Are you trying to say that…"

"Yes." Neel smiled.

"Thirty-six interviews, daddy; I am exhausted," he felt flushed.

"Try thirty-seventh," Neel prompted, "Keep doing what you're doing until you succeed."

Youvik was silent.

At that moment, a piece of biscuit held by Neel broke and fell into his coffee. Riya looked at Youvik. They burst out laughing as soon as their eyes met.

Neel looked at him and picked up another biscuit, *"Only one person can stop me or keep me going; I myself."*

She smirked, "Is that so?"

"I apologize." He said promptly, "Only one person can stop me or keep me going; my wife."

Youvik remembered an email he received the day before while Neel struggled to get the dunked biscuit out of his coffee.

"Good job." Riya said, teasing him.

"I'll try until I succeed," Neel replied confidently.

"No, Daddy," Youvik took his cup back, "Let it be; I want to have coffee; not the biscuit dough."

"I'll get you more," she said as she got up.

"I am good," Neel laughed.

"Okay," Youvik extended his cup towards him, "You can try one last time."

"I am good," Neel patted his shoulder as he got up., "Keep it up."

"For the biscuit rescue mission?" Youvik chuckled.

His father smirked, "You know what that was for."

Youvik smiled and nodded a yes.

"Beware of willpower. It damages your giving-up skills." Neel said before he left.

"Maybe." Youvik nodded. "But where do I get the experience from?"

"Write an article," she suggested.

"On what?"

"On any subject matter of expertise that you claim in the interview that you have."

"And what to do with that write-up."

"Publish it on your blog, social media, or professional websites, as a guest post, etc., and boast about it in the interviewer to prove your off-job experience."

"Sounds like a plan," he smiled.

"But not today," she caressed his head, "You are already exhausted; sleep early, and start fresh tomorrow."

<>

A week later, well into the night, Youvik was again hooked on to his mailbox.

His phone screen flashed, "Monica calling…"

"Hey! How are you?"

"I am cute as always," she chuckled, "How is my baby?"

"Not too bad."

"How about your interviews?"

"Too Bad. They all need an experienced guy."

"Ask them how you can get experience before starting a job."

"Good idea," Youvik smiled, "Next time, I'll ask them."

"If you want, I can do a mock interview to prepare you."

"Some other time, I am tired now," Youvik said as he scrolled through his e-mails.

"Okay, then we'll meet tomorrow at six. At the café next street. The one we went to earlier."

His eyes shot wide open when he saw the new mail. It was from his own email ID.

"Hello!" She checked if the line had gotten disconnected, "Yuvi?"

Youvik was fully engrossed in the mail.

"O, hello? Are you there?"

"Hmm," Youvik murmured as his eyes scanned for the time and date the mail was sent. It was ten days ago.

"All well?"

"No... I mean, yeah."

"One of the best ways to get attention is to write a book titled, 'How to get attention.' So I am planning to write one."

"Hmm."

"What, hmm?"

"Sorry I was lost."

"Tell me, what did I say?"

Youvik murmured, recalling, "Ba... Book."

"Book what?"

"I wish you were a book, and I could say…"

"Say what?"

"Dear book, love you. Librariously yours, Booklover!"

She sighed but didn't reply.

"Good, no?"

"Bye!" She fumed.

Youvik was confused, "What happened, baby?"

"You are ignoring me."

"No, not at all."

"Are you busy chatting with some other girl?"

"Oh God, no."

"Roll up your curiosities in a backpack, go drive, and explore." She lashed.

"Sorry? I didn't understand that."

"Go find a new girlfriend."

"Oho. Baby, I am not ignoring you. I am preparing for my next interview."

"Oopsy."

"Yeah, I was tensed."

"I'm sorry, *babu*. All the best, Sleep on time, and meet me tomorrow at six."

"Sweet dreams. See *ya*."

"Let's fall, or rather rise in Love." She said with a pout.

"Hah. Love *ya*." Youvik smiled.

As she hung up, he quickly pulled the laptop closer and scrolled down. It was similar to the email he had received three years ago from his own e-mail. Bewildered, he scratched his head. He tried to recall if he had used any website to send himself reminders through the own mail. He quickly opened another window and searched, "Phishing through one's own email id."

After skimming a few pages, he jumped back to his email and scrolled down to read.

<>

Dear YOU,

I hope you are going through the journey of life with a lot of perseverance.

I am sure you are doing great at getting a head start in your career, and I wish you all the best for creating a worthy one. Not just you, but everyone has to face tricky and testing situations at some point in their career.

"If the question is monotonousness, the answer is perseverance."

Do you know when you failed that entrance exam? Daddy's thoughtful gesture helped you get back on track. I am not sure if you still remember that, but it will...

<>

"All *Gyan* (preaching)," Youvik said and closed the window without reading any further.

He was quite irritated about his present situation and didn't want to remind himself of it, let alone ponder about it. He turned off the laptop, slid it under the bed, and dozed off.

**

7.

Perseverance

Don't be better than...

◈

Don't be better than any,
but one, your yester-self.

--

A young chap was crying his eyes out as his parents tried hard to console him.

"Good and bad times are like the colours black and white, incomplete without each other," said his father as he patted him.

The kid, still inconsolable, did not react.

"Okay, listen," his father continued, "You wanted an umbrella for school? Let's go and grab one."

They returned home after visiting a few shops. The boy's mother had laid out bowls on the dinner table for the soup. Dinner was ready.

"Where is the TV remote?" She asked as she searched for it.

"No daily soap today," his father announced, looking at his son, "Today is story time."

Receiving no reply from his son, he caressed his head, "It'll be a short one, *Soup-story*."

"What's a soup story?"

"The one that will be over by the time we have soup."

"Hmm," his son noted

"These stories are black and white," his father added, "*Black and white, oldest of the vintages, newest of the last season.*"

"Story, please," the son requested.

"There was a village that had gotten no rainfall for a very long time. All the *Pundits* of the village decided to perform a *Maha-Yagya* (Grand sacrifice) to please *Varuna,* the God of Rain. They decided on a date, gathered all the items required for the *Yagya,* and..."

"It's *Yajna,* not *Yagya,*" the son interrupted.

"Ok, I'll explain that first," his father said as he added some salt to his soup.

"*Yagya* is a Sanskrit dialect that is not easily pronounceable by the people who speak English. They don't have certain syllables in their vocabulary like *Ksha, Tra, Gya,* etc. So they pronounce *Gya* as *Jna* because syllable *Gya* is a combination of syllables *Ja* and *Na;* hence *Yagya* became *Yajna.*"

"Gotcha," his son sighed.

"Now, back to the story." His father continued, "When the D-day arrived, all the villagers gathered at the designated place. They were all empty-handed except a young kid who was hiding something in his hands."

"I know this story," his son interrupted again. "I read it in one of those internet forwards."

The father looked at him and then at his wife, then back at him, "Go on, please."

The son continued, "The child was hiding an umbrella, and when he showed it to the others, they praised his enthusiasm and foresight."

"Okay, and then?"

"Then, nothing, the story ends there. The moral of the story is that we should be optimistic."

"This hashtag, Gen-X generation, flabbergasts me," his father said as he looked at his wife and air-quoted.

"They spend their time in the land of the internet so much that the other side of the story doesn't exist to them."

"I apologize," the chap bowed dramatically, "Please continue your story, your Excellency."

"Better." His father said as he attempted to recall, "So where was I?"

"The kid was hiding something..." prompted his mother.

"Which kid?" he chuckled, "I am old now, so I tend to forget."

The mother shot him a grave look.

"Sorry, Her Highness," he stifled a giggle.

"So," his father continued. "The kid was hiding something, and when they coaxed him to reveal it, he stretched his hands forward."

"*Dumroo* (Pellet drum)?" The *Pundit* asked. People looked on, surprised.

The kid replied innocently, "I have seen villagers play this *dumroo* before ploughing the fields for the new crop a month before it rains. I want to do the same today when we plant the seeds so that it rains after a month, and we can have a good harvest."

"What if it doesn't rain?" Asked the pundit. "And all the seeds die in the soil without water?"

The kid replied with innocence, "We'll plough the fields again and sow another crop for that season."

"And what if it didn't rain in that month, too?" Asked another *Pundit.*

"We'll continue to do it for next season's crop."

"So should we destroy our stock like this?"

"No," the kid smiled. "This way, the soil stays fertile, the farmers will not forget the techniques, and all the bullocks and farmers will remain healthy due to routine work."

"Everyone clapped and praised the kid a lot," his father said proudly.

"That's it?" The boy asked, sipping the last of his soup, "My bowl is empty, and I am hungry."

His father made a face as he looked at his wife, "Pour some more soup, darling. My story is not over yet."

"The villagers continued the practice of ploughing the fields. But even after three months, there was no rain. The villagers believed that the God of Rain, 'Lord *Varuna*' would bring rain to the village only when Lord *Shiva* plays his *dumroo.*"

"The villagers who were so busy with their work did not welcome the Rain God, which offended him. He made Lord Shiva promise him that he would not play his *dumroo* for another two years. That's why the villagers were facing his wrath without even knowing their mistake," he said.

"Oh," the boy became attentive as he realized the twist

in the story.

"They continued the practice of playing the *dumroo* for over four months. Goddess *Paarvati,* the better-half of Lord *Shiva,* was impressed with their trust and faith. Seeing them work tirelessly melted her heart."

"And then?" The son's curiosity piqued.

"She asked Lord Shiva, 'Do you know the villagers are still working so that they don't forget their skills.'

'Tell me something I don't know,' replied Lord *Shiva* while maintaining his *Samadhi.*

'I am sure you must have forgotten one of your skills.' Goddess *Paarvati* remarked.

'Which one?' Lord Shiva quipped.

'The one that you haven't practiced in so long.'

'Be specific.'

'The *Dumroo* is collecting dust. Not sure if it will work like before.'

'It will.'

'Well, not after two years.'

Lord Shiva opened his eyes and looked at *Goddess Paarvati,* 'And why do you think so?'

'I don't just think I know it, and I am sure about it.'

'I am also sure about my skills,' Lord Shiva closed his eyes again.

'Prove it.'

'I don't need to,' Lord Shiva replied, without opening his eyes.

'Well, then, the villagers are better than you.'

'Don't be better than any, but one, your yester-self.' Lord Shiva prompted.

She probed him further, 'Prove it.'

"Lord Shiva lost his calm and opened his eyes. The three *Nadis; Ida, Pingala, and Shushmana* on his forehead turned fiery red and formed a *Trishula*.

Goddess *Paarvati* was not oblivious of the fact. She knew what she was doing. Angry and resentful, Lord Shiva thumped the platform with his hand and then raised it towards the sky. The ground shook with a pulsing thud. The *Dumroo,* tied to his polyvalent weapon, *Trishula,* loosened and, like a crafted piece of iron, flew towards the Lord as if his magical hand had a magnetic force.

Meanwhile, a massive dust storm had swept across the village. All ran to save their family, bullocks, and property from the harsh winds. It all happened in a blink of an eye. Lord Shiva took his eyes off the Goddess, looked at the sky, and closed his eyes. He then rolled the Dumroo on his fingertips.

The skies turned turbulent. The clouds covered the sun. The bright day transformed into a dark evening. The kid stood in the field. His eyes fixed on the sky. The villagers, too, followed his gaze.

Lord Shiva stopped spinning the *dumroo,* and when he did, the ropes tied to it rotated in the air and knocked the pellets so hard that it produced a bolt of lightning that flashed in the clouds. Piercing through the clouds, heading towards the ground, landing straight on the forehead of the kid, the first drop of rain fell.

With a huge thud, billions of droplets fell through the sky, quenching the thirst of the fields and the villagers…"

<>

His father looked at him. The chap sat there with his jaws open in amazement. He snapped his fingers at him.

"Ah oh, sorry, I was lost."

His mother chuckled, "If you are done with your fourth bowl of soup, can we please start with dinner?"

"So, Mr. Hashtag?" Neel quipped as he took a bite. "What did you learn?"

His son crooned, "Moral of the story is..."

"*The only thing that will win you what you want is – perseverance.*" Concluded Neel.

His mother caressed his hair in agreement.

"Ma, your hands are oily!" Youvik chided, waking up from his sleep.

He realized he was dreaming about his past. He was jittery and confused about the connection between the e-mail and a past event. He quickly bent down, pulled the laptop from under the bed and continued reading the rest of the mail.

<>

... The e-mail continued...

Do you know when you failed that entrance exam? Daddy's thoughtful gesture helped you get back on track. I am not sure if you still remember that, but it will help if you recall the lesson. You will realize that it is still very relevant to your life.

Failures only help you get better. Soon you will understand the psyche of your interviewers. You'll learn that it's not important to answer everything correctly. But rather to surprise them with your words and thought process. The story that Daddy had narrated when you were a kid may or may not be a reality check. But the impact that the story creates is deep enough to change your entire approach towards life right now.

The perseverance of villagers showed their dedication to a bigger purpose rather than saving seeds. They focused on learning new techniques of sowing without proper irrigation facilities. They chose to stay active instead of sitting idle and whining about their fate. By doing this, they successfully passed on the art to the next generation.

"You fail not only by not making efforts but also by not learning from your failures."

Keep up your spirits and put on your learning hat. While you wait for the results, do some research on how you can enhance your knowledge. Keep a tab not only on the day-to-day updates but also on the communication skills.

"Prepare for every interview like it's your first. Perform like it's your last."

I wish you all the best for your future endeavours.

Yours truly
YOU

<>

Youvik thought about the old emails and the events that occurred after them.

He was sure that one of his parents was playing a trick on him using the common laptop. They sent him emails from his own ID to motivate him during different phases of his life. He seemed comfortable and more confident, and ready to face his life struggles.

He decided that he was not going to let his parents know that he knew their little secret.

<>

After his morning rituals, Youvik headed straight to his father's room.

"I'll be like the villagers," Youvik announced peeping in. His parents were clueless about what he just said.

"Do you remember the story you told me when I had failed the entrance exam?"

"Who? Me?" Neel, "Which one?"

"You are old now," Youvik chuckled, "I'll score my century."

He scratched his head and looked at his wife, all confused, "Which story, Ma'am?"

"Lord Shiva and the villagers," she smirked as she

folded the blanket.

"Oh yes yes and the moral of the story was," Neel added, *"Five Ups of life - Buckle up, Start up, Keep it up, Don't give up, Cheer up."*

"Well, last time it was something else," Youvik said amused, He could hear them laugh as he left.

**

8.

Un-crumple

Life and people are always...

◈

Life and people are always
gung-ho to crush you,
so Learn to un-crumple yourself.

--

An older man was walking briskly in the lobby at office. He was holding a bunch of papers in one hand and a laptop in another. As soon as he entered the meeting room, all the team members got up.

"Guys!" He exclaimed. "We are not meeting our deadlines. Can anyone care to explain why?"

"Sir, we were not equipped to deal with it. Also, we get enough time to discuss it with the stakeholders." One of the team members replied.

"And you think those excuses are justified?"

"Sir," Youvik raised his hand. "We had strict deadlines."

"Then why did we accept this assignment?"

"We had no other projects. So we were forced to accept it."

"What's the antonym of 'Yes'?"

"No," he replied.

"What was stopping you from saying this two-letter word?"

No one dared to respond.

"Instead of not delivering what you had promised, you could have just said NO." The older man chided as he walked out of the room.

<>

It was two years since Youvik started his first job. He juggled several tasks at once. He worked on assignments and was always behind deadlines. He tried to grasp the know-how of his job, but he never got to learn it in the copy-paste world of corporate training.

"Monica calling." Youvik's mobile flashed.

He answered the call.
"Movie night?" She asked him.
"Baby, I am swamped today."
"I don't know anything. Six means six."
"But I...." before he could say anything, she hung up.

<>

"God. It's four already." Youvik sighed, looking at the time.
He leaned back in his chair, sipping his coffee.

"And we are taking our first break just now." Amit, one of his colleagues nodded and said. "It feels so good to step away from the screen for a while."
"This is getting monotonous and boring. Doing the

same work every day."

"Ever thought of starting a business?"

Youvik sighed, "Have to search for an opportunity."

Amit quoted. "Opportunities do not come in fancy wrappers; only toffees do, which give temporary contentment. Toil to unwrap the real one covered in hardships."

"Went over the top," Youvik nodded. "Tell me in simple words if you have a plan."

"I think we need more than just a plan. We need steps."

"True that."

Amit smiled, *"Idea-less steps and step-less ideas are the greatest wastes."*

"Again," Youvik smiled, "Have you subscribed any website for quotations?"

"Not website, but reading a book these days titled," he smiled, "10 Golden steps of life."

Just then, their boss joined them at their bay, murmuring furiously.

"You seem tense, Parv. What is it?" Youvik asked him.

Parv looked at both of them and fumed, "When you hold a kid above your head, the first thing the kid will do is kick you in your face."

Youvik looked at Amit.

Parv added, "I did everything for your teammate's promotion, and he bloody complained against me to the HR."

"Sir." Amit attempted to console him. "Calm down. Have a seat."

Parv pulled the chair and sat on table putting his foot on the chair.

"Sir, take this," he gave him a blank paper. "Tear it for me."

"But… why?" Parv was bewildered.

"Just do it, sir, and vent out your anger."

He went ahead and tore it in wrath.

"Now," Amit grabbed another piece of paper. "Crumple this one as much as you can."

Parv crushed it with his fist and threw it towards him.

"Feeling better?"

He nodded. "I wish I could do this to him."

"Now," said Amit, tossing it back to him. "Try to tear it without un-crumpling."

He tried a couple of times but couldn't.

Youvik understood the message and smiled at him.

Amit beamed. "If the world pulls you down, be as unbothered as a crumpled paper. Then nobody can tear you apart."

"Good one," Parv remarked, getting up. "Let me crumple up that idiot."

As soon as he left, Youvik praised him. "Good example."

"Example was good, but not the lesson."

"Sorry?" Youvik was confused.

"The actual lesson was..." he turned to Youvik. "*Learn to un-crumple yourself, for life, and people are always gung-ho to crush you."*

"Good one but I think he misunderstood it."

"Hah, that was all *Gyan,"* Amit chuckled. "Our boss was that kid who once kicked his boss. History repeats itself."

Youvik was taken aback. "I fail to understand this corporate world and related politics."

Amit smirked. *"Corporate world has dirtiest cooks, serving the cleanest ever politics."*

"True that."

<>

"Life is all about Takeaways, from great people and Giveaways to the needy ones." Youvik said, mimicking the hero's voice. "Why the hell on earth did you want to watch this film?"

"How dare you say anything about my favourite actor," Monica retorted. "I'll carve a dimple on your bum forever."

"Our mechanic is really good with dents." Youvik chuckled.

"Very funny."

"I am hungry?" Youvik said as he held his growling stomach, "Shall we have something?"

"No," she gave him a quick hug. "I am going on a dinner date."

He raised an eyebrow. "Breakup after a movie?"

"Don't worry," she laughed. "I'll give you a three-week' notice before I break up."

"You are crazy!"

"So is my cousin. And she is coming over for a night out."

"Cool. I leave my work for you, and you already have plans with other people."

"Her plan came as a complete surprise. Sorry, but I can't ditch her."

"Fine," he hugged her and held her close to him. "But can't you stay for some time?" She blushed at his unexpected request. They spent some time together in his car before he dropped her home.

**

9.

Defocus

Ctrl Alt Del...

◈

Ctrl Alt Del
for humans would mean;
Take Control,
Opt Alternatives,
Delete Fears.

--

It was a typical day at work for Youvik. He was at the coffee machine getting a refill when his mobile chimed. He pulled it out to find yet another mail from his own email ID.

<>

Dear YOU,

You might ignore this mail, but it'll be for your own good if you didn't. A seminar 'Say No; when, why, to whom' will soon be conducted in the amphitheatre of your office complex. It would be best if you attended it not because it's free, but because you need to learn the art of saying no.

Yours truly,
YOU

<>

Youvik ground his teeth in frustration. "I wish I could tell you how hard I want to hit you in the eye."

"Sorry?" His manager, Parv, peeked from behind.

"Uh, sorry, Parv, I was talking to myself." Youvik smiled sheepishly.

Parv was about to leave the cafe when he suddenly turned around and said,

"By the way, one suggestion,"

"Yes, please."

"You should attend that seminar." He smiled, "It is scheduled for next to next Monday."

Youvik's brows curved into a frown as he realized that Parv was peeking into his phone.

"Sure," he said, rather annoyed.

Youvik murmured something as he saw Parv leave. He sat down to sip his coffee.

"Tell me one thing."

Youvik was startled to see Parv again.

"Sure, go on."

"Only the seniors know about the seminar." He scratched his head. "How come you got a mail?"

"Umm," Youvik was clueless, too. "I don't know."

"The speaker might have sent it to all the employees," Parv shrugged.

Once Parv left, Youvik pulled out his mobile and

rechecked the email. "Not sure if Mom and Dad are spying on me at work, too. When will I be able to crack this puzzle."

<>

"Rugged interior in hotels, lavish one in huts - the irony," remarked Monica, observing the café's interior.

Later that evening, they went out on a coffee date.

"Yeah," Youvik looked around. "They got it done recently."

"A beautiful girl is sitting in front of you, and you are looking around."

"Ha ha," he looked at her. *"Coffee is to love, what guitar is to a song."*

"You never fail to impress me with your perfectly timed one-liners," Monica smiled. "Anyway, will you attend that seminar?"

"No," Youvik picked up the pastry. "It's after office hours, and I would be down with Monday blues."

"Dude," said Tinku, tapping on his shoulder.

"How on earth did you find out about our dating place?" Giggled Youvik.

"Helloz," Monica made a cutesy face at the service guys. "One more coffee, please."

"It's self-service here." Youvik reminded her.

"Please get one for me too." Tinku winked at him.

Youvik's protests went unheard. He ended up serving them.

They chatted for an hour before they were ready to leave.

The moment the bill arrived, Tinku got up.

"Excuse me. I need to go to the loo."

Monica jingled, looking at Youvik. "*Beware of friends who go pee, when they see, the bill.*"

Youvik went to the counter and paid the bill.

When he came back to the table, Tinku was narrating yet another story. "So she said.."

"I am leaving.

Where?

Not where but whom.

Whom?

'You.'"

Youvik stood there, looking at him.

"What?"Tinku rolled his eyes.

"Which girlfriend are you talking about?"

"The first one, obviously," he said, looking at Monica.

"What about the other five before that *first one*?"He asked as they walked out of the restaurant.

"Oh, that? Then it was the eighth. Four ditched me. I befriended all their besties and then ditched all four. Total eight but *Hisaab barabar* (revenge balanced)."

Monica looked at him, "*Who wants to stay, will, no matter what; who doesn't, won't; no matter what.*"

He snapped his finger, "Point."

<>

"Good evening, everyone. Before I introduce myself,

let me quickly ask you a question."

"What would you do if you knew that you would NOT fail?"

"Well, many things." He said and nodded at the audience.

"Now tell me..." he adjusted his tie. "What would you do if you knew that you WILL fail?"

The host of the seminar continued.

"Or, let's put it this way...."

"What would you do if you knew that your journey was not worth your efforts or time?

The answer is a no-brainer– 'nothing.' You should not do anything if it doesn't have a silver lining for you. The take here is to say 'no' to certain things in life, especially to those people who might be closest to you or are your seniors at work.

You guessed it right. Today we shall explore how to say 'no' with confidence and not feel as if you're obliged to agree to everything."

The speaker adjusted the microphone. "My name is Tony and I have spent nearly half my life specializing in 'Learning and Personnel Development.' I have also written extensively on subjects such as Improving Habits, Leadership, Performance Management, etc. And, no, I am not here to sell my books. Don't worry."

He winked at a few people seated in the front row.

"But do visit my website and buy a few billion copies of my books."

There was a laughter riot, and Youvik was among them.

"Saying NO is an art; master it."

"Sir," a girl raised a hand, "What if we stay silent?"

"Well then," he chuckled, *"Staying silent is a skill, knowing when and where is an art."*

"What if I talk something else, rather than saying no?"

"Talking is a skill; what, when and how to talk is an art." The audience laughed.

"What if I speak it up that I don't want it?"

"Speaking up is a skill; what, when and how to talk is an art."

"Then how to say no?" All laughed again.

"Ok, I'll reword my first phrase," he smiled, *"Saying no is a skill; when and how to say no is an art. Master that art."*

"When to say no?" The guy sitting next to her hid his face while all laughed again.

"It depends entirely on the situation you are in. If you think you would sound rude or are afraid of the consequences, then work on it."

"Thank you."

"Thank you to you too. Now, moving further, tell me all, which key combination do you use to restart your computer?"

"Control + Alt + Delete." The audience replied in chorus.

"Ctrl Alt Del for humans would mean 'Take Control, Opt Alternatives, and Delete Fears.' Agree?"

All nodded.

"It's a degree, be a student and, if possible, master it. You'll be there one day. Here are a few considerations before saying 'no.'

One. Always be polite while saying 'no.' If that's not an option; at least maintain a neutral tone.

Two. If you think it's feasible, then explain the reason for declining the offer. However, you are not bound to do so every time for everyone.

Three. Convey your message effectively in words..."

<>

Youvik's mobile chimed. He pulled it and found a text from Monica.

"Where are you?"

"Amphitheatre," he replied.

"Aren't you supposed to be down with Monday blues?"

"I'm trying to learn the art of saying 'no' to people who ask me to bring them coffee."

"LOL. Bye."

<>

"Fear of saying NO refrains you from saying it altogether." Tony continued.

"Don't be afraid of saying NO. Be brave and face the waves because..." He looked at the text on the projector screen. *"Waves are not as dangerous as the fear of waves."*

"Here are a few reasons owing to which you find yourself unable to say 'no' -

One. You feel guilty about rejecting someone.

Two. You are conscious about 'What if they think I'm rude.'

Three. You do not want to hamper your future dealings with that person.

Once you have analyzed all the possibilities and have done your homework, you might be determined to say 'no.'

But how to word it?

The politest way is just to say 'Sorry.'

Different countries have different cultures. For example, in the UK, the most common method of expressing 'no' is 'I am afraid.'

Another one that I came across was, 'I would love to...but....'

Here is a compilation of various options to choose from. No. Sorry or I am so sorry. My apologies. I would love to, but... Maybe next time. Not as of now. Tough for me. I am occupied; Oh please etc.

'Oh please' is too casual; use it at your own risk."

All laughed aloud.

"These suggestions are only useful if you are determined not to let anyone walk over you."

"So, my friends," he looked at everyone, his arms wide open. "There is another perspective to NO."

He concluded his seminar. *"Defocus, for there lays another perspective."*

<>

Youvik was so occupied with work that he didn't even notice Parv was standing behind him.

"I think you have gotten a friend request," Parv whispered.

Youvik gave a little squeak of surprise.

"I am sorry that I startled you." Parv chuckled.

"Ha, ha. Hi, Parv. I didn't see you come in."

"Only when you give your best to what you do will you get what you desire," Parv said pompously.

"Sorry," Youvik felt embarrassed. "I was so submerged in work that I forgot to turnoff the notifications."

"Never mind. I thought that's your gym trainer." Parv chuckled.

"Oh, no, no, that may be a random friend request."

"Good. Anyway, can you come to the office this Saturday?

"Sorry." The entire team said in a chorus.

"Haha, looks like all you guys attended the seminar," he smiled and left.

"Such a snooping dog," Amit whispered.

"Break?"Youvik asked him, and they left for the cafe.

On his way to the cafe, he checked his phone. And there it was, another email.

As he was about to open the mail, his colleague from another team bumped into him. "Dude, how are you? Long time, no see?"

And they continued their chat.

Later in the day Youvik was so occupied in work that he forgot to check his email.

**

10.

Transform

Sunshine, external, is universal...

◈

Sunshine, external, is universal;
internal, the eternal.
Choose and shine.

--

Youvik was yawning while working on his laptop. He was sitting on his bed.

"You are drowning in work." Riya was standing by his room door. "Your body is signalling you to sleep."

"Hmm. This is submission week Ma."

"Sleep on time, baby."

"Almost done, dude. You go to sleep."

"Okay. Good night."

He quickly completed his work and went to brush his teeth.

He brushed his teeth with one hand. In the other, he held his mobile and scrolled through it. Then he remembered the mail notification, and his eyes shot wide open upon reading the mail.

<>

Dear YOU,

I hope you are doing well.

This email is regarding the friend request you received yesterday. You haven't responded to it yet. I'm assuming it is because it's from an unknown person.

Let me give you a hint - The chopstick.

Yours Truly,
YOU

<>

This time it was different. Instead of trying to get to the bottom of this maze, his mind was racing to recollect memories. "Chopstick?..."

"Slept?" A text flashed on his phone.

Youvik smiled. It was a message from Monica. He plopped himself down on his bed and texted back, "*All that doesn't let me sleep; is my coffee or you.*"

"Nice. Now recharge my mobile."

Youvik called her. "I always call you, then how do you run out of talk- time?"

"Okay. Bye."

"Sorry, sorry," Youvik chuckled, and they chatted for a while.

"Hey! You remember Monty?" She quipped.

"Who?"

"Our classmate back in school days?"

"Amm..."

"That chap with a skinny physique and a protuberant Adam's apple. It even earned him the nickname 'chopstick.'"

"Oh yeah. That guy." Youvik paused to think. Was it Monica who hacked his mailbox? Was she sending him all those e-mails?

"He seems to have transformed himself."

Youvik was still lost in his thoughts.

"Yuvu."

"Sorry. Network issues."

"I said, he has transformed."

"Oh yeah, he sent me a friend request a few days back. He looks like a gym trainer."

"Oh, yeah. I feel bad for the nickname we gave him."

"I know, but he was comfortable with that name. Sometimes he didn't respond if we called him Monty." Youvik giggled.

"Haha. Anyway, is this your agenda for this lovely mid-night chat?"

"No, baby. I was just replying to your..."

"Shut up. Tell me something about me."

"Oh yeah, I have one for you."

"Too much of - Oh Yeah. Your parents will kick you out of the house."

"And I'll get a reason to meet you."

They laughed and continued talking.

<>

Youvik was on the way to his office the next morning.

He accepted the friend request and sent a message. "Hi, Monty."

"You rascal!" Monty was quick to respond. "When did you start addressing me by my name? You guys always called me Chopsticks."

He felt bad about his silly behaviour. They exchanged their mobile numbers. Youvik called him.

"I guess you should thank all of us. Didn't we motivate you to become what you are now?" Youvik giggled.

"Yeah, thanks. But I have always been a fitness freak. Even then, I had six-pack abs but no muscle mass. Only two of my very close friends knew that I had been going to the gym since the tenth standard." Monty replied.

"Oh! Your coaching mates, right?"

"Yes. I was simultaneously managing my hyperactive body type, thyroid, and a myriad of other problems. I was always told that I could never build a bulky body."

"So, what pushed you to achieve this?" Youvik sounded curious.

"After college, I got an internship. On the side, I researched my body type, diet routines and gained knowledge on how I can transform myself." Monty narrated.

"Then I read a few success stories on the net. Some of them were in a much worse situation when they began. It gave me immense confidence and hope. Next, I made a list of coaches near me and looked into their blogs and reviews. I contacted five of them and explained what I wanted to achieve." Monty paused to take a breath.

"Okay, then?" Youvik was excited.

"My goal was to achieve a natural transformation with minimum food supplements."

"It must have been quite a task," Youvik remarked.

"I weighed all the pros and cons before making the final decision. I didn't want to commit to a particular gym on the very first go. So, I put out a clause that I'll try their services for a month and then decide whether to continue with them." Monty concluded.

"Good move, man. Most people can't keep up and end up quitting. So, how did you keep at it?" Youvik probed further.

"Honestly, hitting the gym was very tough during the first month.The trainer would never let me do the exercises that I preferred. So after the fourth week, I decided to discontinue and workout with another trainer." He laughed.

"My trainer used to say," Monty added, *"Let your feelings dream, dreams act, actions speak."*

"Eventually, I got the whole picture. His actions spoke. He was just helping me build my stamina through cardio. It prepared my body for rigorous weight training in the coming months." Monty continued.

"Right," Youvik prompted.

"In the following six months, results had started to show. He had trained and equipped me with enough clever tips so that I could start on my own. When I would be tired in my last reps, my trainer would say - *"Remember someone you hate while you exercise."* And I would do one more rep with extra weights."

"You are an inspiration, Monty!" Youvik lauded him. "So, where have you opened your gym?"

"Sorry?"

"Gym. You must have opened one to help and motivate others."

"They say..." He laughed. *"Don't judge a cover by the book. All know this quote is wrong; still, they judge."*

"Sorry?"

"Stereotypes," he chuckled. "You think I look like a gym trainer, so I must have opened my own gym."

"Oh, no no… not exactly," Youvik laughed. "Actually, yes."

"Haha! Anyway, the name of my venture is Chopsticks and Tadka."

"Oh." Youvik was astonished. "That's great, and may I know the specialty?"

"*Hor ki* (Obviously), full on *Punjabi*." He went on. "And I want you to like and follow the page on all socials. Do visit me whenever you have time. I'll serve you something special."

"*Bhai saab! Eh vi koi puchan wali gall ae?* (*Bro*! Is it a thing to ask?)"

"Thanks, I always wanted to have my own restaurant. I loved cooking."

"That's great! You are living your dream. I am so proud of you. You're doing so well in life."

"But the biggest challenge was my looks."

"Ahem."

"People expect you to justify your profession by your looks, especially by your bodyweight."

"That's somewhat true."

"A chef or a restaurant owner or, for that matter, a manager in your office has to look like a boss and not like a teenage boy."

"Body-shaming for skinnier ones is very much there but no one is concerned about it; no one cares."

"True that."

"Yeah; so changing my whole outlook was my priority. Unfortunately, I didn't get the desired effect when I joined the gym in school days. I realized the mistakes that I had been repeating for years. I would have continued making them if I didn't chance upon a mentor. The reason I'm telling you this is because every one of us needs to dispel our ignorance and accept our follies. We should not only be willing to learn but also unlearn. If this is paired with perseverance, no force can stop you."

"Hmm. So you became shining star, internally and externally."

Monty smiled, "*Sunshine, external, is universal; internal, the eternal. Choose and shine.*"

"True that."

"Okay, enough about me. What have you been up to?" Monty asked.

"Aah, First job; new office, good salary, so far so good."

"Great."

"Maybe I should also start working out," he laughed. "So that I also look bossy and get promoted."

"Ha ha, why not. I am always there to help. *Let the success be the voice of whispering hard-work.*"

"Cool, see you soon. I will visit your restaurant with my parents someday."

"Any time, bro." He hung up.

Youvik toiled at work the whole day. His day ended with sharing his day's summary with Monica over late night calls.

**

11.

Unlearn

Home-Work grew up...

◈

Home-Work grew up
and became
Work-From-Home.

--

"Get curd from the refrigerator," Riya called out. She was serving breakfast.

Youvik made a sour face. "Can I get something other than yogurt today?"

"Mr. Hashtag!" Neel looked at him. "What is the difference between curd and yogurt?"

Youvik looked into the emptiness and nodded with a no.

"I know." Riya prompted. "Curd got hurt while doing yoga, hence Yog-hurt."

They both giggled, and Youvik rolled his eyes. "Anyway, I am changing my breakfast habits from today."

"And why is this change happening?" She asked.

"See." Youvik showed her Monty's picture.

"OMG. Is that Monty?" She stared at the picture with wonder and astonishment.

"Yeah. He sent me a friend request. At first, I thought he was one of those fitness freaks who wanted to get more followers."

"He has transformed."

Neel leaned in to have a look. "Show me."

"Yup," Youvik nodded. "After talking to Monty, I realized that the possibility of what you want to achieve not only depends on you, but also on the approach that you take and the strategies you use."

"Sounds like you two had a *philosophically repetitious* conversation." She smiled.

"He told me all about his transformation journey. He did full-fledged research before settling for his trainer because, ultimately, he would be the one to bring the best out of him. He also stressed the importance of having a mentor."

"Indeed. A mentor guides you through the dos and don'ts," she added.

"He helped me decode the secret of success."

"Lovely," she smiled.

"I'll take you both to his restaurant."

"Restaurant?" Neel remarked in astonishment. "I thought he opened a gym."

"Stereotypes." Youvik chuckled.

<>

"Guys, we have to submit the code by today," Parv said as he sipped his coffee.

Youvik was at his office. He was working with his whole team.

"But there are a few hurdles, and then there is the paucity of time," Youvik added.

"Don't we have the capacity of six man-days?" Parv added.

"Agree, but we can't proceed without any replies to our queries," *Iti* replied.

"Let's see," Parv replied, gazing at her.

"And it's person-days, not man-days." She prompted.

"My apologies. I am sure that you guys will stay back and complete all tasks by today." Parv smiled and left.

Amit looked at him. "He does nothing other than sipping coffee."

"And checking out girls," added *Iti*. "Such a *perv*."

Amit added, "*Corporate irony; you will see the best of machines and worst of people.*"

Youvik did not take his eyes off his system. "I wish this company had a three-sixty degree appraisal system."

"As if it made a difference in companies that have one," she replied furiously typing on keyboard.

<>

Youvik was in the cafe with his team at lunch when his phone chimed.

"You have got a job offer mail," giggled Amit.

"Hah, I wish." He said, picking up his mobile to find another mail from his own ID.

<>

Dear YOU,

Invite Mr. Singh for coffee. He has a hidden treasure related to time that needs to be shared with the world. Request him to publish his masterpiece, titled '7-8-9' under a weekly column called - *"And thou win."*

P.S. Refrain from letting him know that you are aware of him being a columnist.

Yours truly,
YOU

<>

He slid the phone back into his pocket. Post lunch, the whole team was back to work at their desks.

It was 5:30 pm by the time Youvik clicked the SUBMIT button. "Final report is also gone."

Just then, Parv walked in. "Guys, as discussed, we will stretch today."

"But our work is done." A team member protested.

"I will review your files."

"But these are submitted to the regulators," added Youvik.

"I will still review. Book your cabs late today. I'll approve it." He picked up his coffee mug and left for the cafeteria.

Iti got up and followed him.

"Today, she'll leave on time." Amit whispered.

<>

After ten minutes, *Iti* came back and started packing her bag. "See ya guys. I'll login from home."

"So who is not well today? Kid or husband?" Amit asked.

"Father-in-law," she said smiling.

As she was about to leave, Parv came in. "I just spoke to your father-in-law. He seems fine."

She looked at him in shock.

"So we have six man-days now." Parv smiled. "Oh, I am sorry. Six person-days."

Iti clenched her jaw unwrapping her laptop.

"Don't be surprised," Parv added. "I saved your husband's number the last time he called to say that he was not well and needed you to take an off from work."

She looked at the team in shock.

"Get back to work, guys. I'll review it at 7 pm." He left for the cafe.

"I wish I could tell him," *Iti* fumed. *"Dear Boss! Don't be a boss-hole."*

<>

At the dinner table, Neel arranged the bowls and served soup.

"YOU!" Riya called out. "Reports not yet submitted?"

"Coming," Youvik shouted back from his room.

As the family settled down for dinner, Neel said, "I have a story to tell today."

"Quick, please, I have loads of work," Youvik said before slurping his soup.

"I too have a story," smiled Riya. "Short one. Just a one-liner."

"Ahem," Neel raised his brow.

"Home-Work grew up and became Work-From-Home."

"Good one," Neel laughed out aloud. "I also have one. *'Work-life balance is like the colours black and white; appropriately proportioned to perfection.'* How is this one?"

Youvik rolled his eyes at them. "You guys are too much."

"Let's go to a movie this Saturday." Riya suggested.

"Dude! I am planning to invite Mr. Singh for coffee this Saturday evening." Youvik said, sipping his soup.

"Your English teacher?" Neel enquired.

"Yup."

"Out of the blue?"

"Yup."

"He is a nobleman." Neel added. "He helped that poor chap Bunty."

"Bunty?" Riya asked.

"Yuvi's old classmate, one of the backbenchers."

"Oh, yeah." Youvik nodded.

"He got his father a driver's job at some millionaire's home."

"Nice."

<>

It was a Saturday evening. Youvik was whisking coffee. "Sorry, sir, we couldn't talk much that day."

"That's okay," Mr. Singh smiled and pointed at the coffee. "Happy to see you being independent. You must have learned it from your Mom."

"Nope." Youvik looked at the coffee mug. "Dad taught me."

"Wonderful."

"I want to learn and do so many things, but I'm struggling to meet my own expectations."

"Certainly, you will, my son," Mr. Singh smiled. *"Learn. Unlearn. Repeat."*

"Fingers crossed." Youvik poured some hot milk into the cup.

Mr. Singh laughed. "I am aware of the daily trials you youngsters have."

"Sat Shri Akaal (God is truth and Timeless); *Veer Ji* (Brother)." Riya touched Mr. Singh's feet.

"Sat Shri Akaal; Puttar," Mr. Singh raised his hands to bless her. "God bless you."

She laid out some biscuits on the table and handed over a newspaper to Youvik. "Here, you asked for it. And I am heading for my computer class. Okay, *Veer Ji.*"

"Okay, dude," Youvik said.

Realizing that Mr. Singh noticed him, he consciously corrected himself. "Ma. Okay, Ma."

After serving coffee to Mr. Singh, Youvik pulled up a chair.

"I never find time to do all the things that I wish to do."

Mr. Singh's gaze fell on the newspaper that was placed on the table.

"Sir?"

"Yes?" Mr. Singh looked at him, clueless.

"I need your help."

Mr. Singh did not respond. Instead, he leaned forward and picked up the newspaper. *"Irony; we want our handwriting to look like typed fonts and our computer fonts to look like handwritten text."*

"True that." Youvik smiled.

He started folding the corners. "There is a way you can manage time."

"Yes, please." Youvik sat up attentively.

After thinking for a while, Mr. Singh continued. "You do know how your examinations have a set timeline and that they cover your entire syllabus. It is a meticulous process."

Youvik was puzzled but still gave a slight nod.

"Everything that you did while studying is called 'time-boxing.' It means following a timetable, no matter how difficult it is."

"The reason behind failures is not only that we didn't have a plan. The reason is that we didn't time-box the plan." Mr. Singh connected the dots for Youvik.

"True that, sir; out of school, out of discipline."

Youvik was even more attentive.

"It happens with everyone, son. Don't feel guilty. I'll tell you a trick."

"Do you remember how you used to wake up on time for college? The answer is setting the alarm. Some people even put two alarms with a ten-minute interval before the final one."

"*Bhai saab* (bro). I also do that." Youvik giggled and realized what he had just said. "Sorry, I mean amazing."

"It's alright. Some even set the alarm an hour before as an extra step to trick the subconscious mind into sleeping for only one hour once the alarm goes off." Mr. Singh chuckled.

"Is it?" Youvik offered him some snacks. "But sir…"

"Wait. Let me finish."

"Sorry, sir."

"An alarm is the best way to stick to plans."

"Agree."

"It may sound funny, but…." Mr. Singh smiled, "Set three alarms in a day - 7 pm, 8 pm, and 9 pm and label it using an action word. For example, if your goal is to write a book or develop an app, then use action texts like 'WRITE NOW' or 'DEVELOP.' You can even make use of a code word so that no one else would be able to understand."

"Sounds like a plan." Youvik nodded, sipping his coffee.

"Initially, these alarms will be irritating. You might even procrastinate."

"But for the obvious."

"But gradually..." Mr. Singh continued, "You will get

into the habit of practicing your goal at least once a day."

Youvik picked up his phone. "Let me set these alarms right away."

"At the beginning, you would probably spend just ten minutes on your plan. But that will soon increase to fifteen or twenty minutes, and eventually, you will see yourself working on your passion for three hours at a stretch."

Youvik looked at him in awe. Passion gleamed in his large brown eyes.

"The reason behind the timings is whether you are a student, an employee, or a freelancer; you would always be able to squeeze out some time from even your busiest schedule."

Seeing Youvik yearning for more, he added, "Let me explain this. Assume that you are swamped with either office work or studies. I would still suggest that you set a reminder. Today, tomorrow, the day after, weeks or months later, someday in the future, you will tell yourself that it's enough and you need to work on your plan."

"Bomb," Youvik smiled and then realized the language he used and corrected himself. "I mean mind-blowing. Your mind has always been a treasure of revolutionary ideas."

"Goal-setting, without a time-boxed plan, becomes time-bomb; it just explodes."

"True that, sir."

"Thank you, son." Mr. Singh smiled. "But I am old now. I have started forgetting things. I want you youngsters to extract and learn as much as you can from me, at the earliest."

"Ha ha ha," Youvik blurted out, picking up the newspaper. "Then why don't you resume your column-writing once again?"

"Hah," Mr. Singh chuckled. "Now, I am an old fellow. Who would be interested in my old-school preaching?"

"I am serious. Write about this masterpiece *'7-8-9' under the section called....*" Youvik looked straight into his eyes. *"And thou win."*

Mr. Singh envisaged his piece of work gaining fame worldwide.

"One second." Mr. Singh frowned. "How do you know that I used to write columns under that section?"

Youvik realized that he had goofed up. He was at a loss for words.

"Youvik?"Mr. Singh asked, looking at Youvik with a stern look, expecting an answer.

"Arr... baaaa... Bunty told me."

"Who?"

"Ha ha. Now I understand, sir. Your age really is making you forget things." Youvik said. "You had gotten his father a driver's job at a rich household."

"Oh, right, my bad." Mr. Singh smiled.

Youvik let out a sigh of relief.

"But...." Mr. Singh prompted again. "I don't think I ever told him about my columns."

"Sir," Youvik giggled. "Now, I am entirely convinced of your poor memory."

"Anyways." Mr. Singh chuckled. "The newspaper

changed the column's title to – '*Just win. Period*'. I actually follow them regularly."

They continued talking for a long time sharing their views and thoughts.

<>

An hour later Mrs. Verma came back home.

"Having fun?" She smiled as she entered the house.

"Dude." Youvik took the grocery bag from her and quickly corrected himself. "Ma! Let me help you."

"Programmers guide?" Mr. Singh pointed at the book she was holding.

Mr. Singh laughed and continued. "You probably have no idea of the genius your Mom is."

"Is she?" Youvik peeped at the book. "Sorry. I mean, I know she is. But is it?"

"Yes." Mr. Singh nodded. "She once solved a complex programming code that was in the *Sanskrit* language."

Riya smiled. "If it weren't you, *Veer Ji,* to motivate me, I wouldn't have pursued my silly theories."

"Oh, you never told me this, Ma." Youvik gazed at her in awe.

"Yeah," Mr. Singh added. "She was also writing that thesis about coding in Sanskrit. I forgot the title."

"Ma, when were you planning to tell me?"

"You never bothered to check, baby, about what I was working on." She replied. "And what you also don't know is that it's in *Sanskrit.* It's a lot better, easier and powerful than any other scripting language in the world. Including the cross-platform and cross-lingual compatibility."

Youvik looked at her in awe.

"I agree," prompted Mr. Singh. "But I forgot the title."

"It's okay, Veer Ji. You tend to forget things. Anyway, I got this book for cleaning the virus that has hit our computer." She said. "I'll get some sweets for you."

Mr. Singh laughed as Youvik teased him for his forgetfulness. "Ma! Did you know that sir was a columnist for a newspaper?"

"I know," she nodded. "His daughter and I used to clip the paper cuttings and paste them in a diary."

"Yeah," Mr. Singh mimicked Youvik's style. "I remember that."

"Wow," Youvik shrugged. "You never told me any of this. Am I not your son?"

She pinched his chin. "You never asked, baby."

Mr. Singh laughed and got up. "I'll take your leave now. Today was one of the best evenings of my life."

"Thank you, Mr. Singh. You always give him the best guidance, do visit us again." Riya wished him a fond farewell.

"My teacher used to tell us…." Mr. Singh said. "*Light-up lives or be the reason.*"

Youvik went towards his scooter. "I'll drop you home, sir."

**

12.

Journey

Go solo...

◈

Go solo;
be it a trip,
be it a search,
with or for,
yourself.

--

"Why am I obeying some random person's orders? If I hadn't motivated Mr. Singh, would it have made any difference today?" Youvik thought to himself with his eyes shut tight.

The next morning, he lay awake on his bed, pondering over the strange e-mails. Everything that was happening seemed like an eternity.

"Can you please go out and buy bread for breakfast?" Riya asked as she entered his room.

"Good morning to you too." Youvik reached for his mobile and saw that it was 7:00 AM.

"Quick."

"Just five minutes more." Youvik closed his eyes again.

He got up reluctantly, brushed his teeth, took the money from his wallet, and went to the market. He was buying bread when it started pouring.

The next moment water splashed on his face. Wiping his face, he noticed his mother was standing next to his bed with an empty glass in her hand.

"Ma! It was so cold." He pulled the bed sheet over his head.

She pulled it away from him. "I can pour hot water if you want."

"I just asked for 5 minutes." He said, reaching his mobile, "Oh hell! It's nine?"

She nodded. "Thanks for the information."

"I was…"

She gave him a death stare and headed towards the kitchen. "Just yesterday, Mr. Singh taught you how to manage time. And you failed on the first day itself."

"Sorry, I was reading a blog last night and lost track of time." Youvik got up, rubbing his eyes. He scrambled towards the living room.

Sitting down at the dining table, he yawned loudly. "Dude, what's for breakfast?"

"Scolding." Riya replied, nestling on the couch with her coffee. "You want it fried or toasted?"

"Sorry for today, Ma. Tomorrow onwards, I'll follow the timetable."

"Amen." Neel joined them.

"Dad, you know sometimes it happens that you think you did something, but it was actually a dream?"

"It's called lucid dreaming." Neel smiled.

"Yeah, I know."

"And people use the powerful technique of lucid dreaming to improve themselves and to achieve their dreams. Not to sleep for another hour." Riya fumed.

"I am trying." Youvik nodded. He unlocked his phone. He straightened up as he saw another email.

<>

Dear YOU,

I hope you are doing fine.

I will get to the point; you will have something very special with someone very special today.

Yours truly,
You

<>

"Who's the special one?" Youvik wondered aloud, and then he looked at his mother.

"Don't look at me if you need money. You won't get it." Riya opened her programming book and began reading.

"Ma," he grinned and walked over to her.

"Don't you dare take my coffee." Riya said, underlining the text in the book with a pencil.

"I wasn't going to," he chuckled and picked up the newspaper from the table.

"As a punishment, make your own coffee and

breakfast today."

"How a mother can watch her son going weak from hunger," he said, pretending to read the newspaper. "Dad, is there anything for me to eat?"

"You know, in space, along with black holes, there are white holes as well, but I don't have any time to explore them today as I have to wash clothes." Neel got up to leave.

"Universe is changing," Youvik slow clapped. "And so are the husbands."

Neel chimed. *"Black and white seem like a journey into space which is destined back to earth."*

"Not again, Dad."

After a minute, Riya went into the kitchen and came back with a plateful of food.

Youvik looked up at her, trying not to laugh, "What?"

"Learn to hold the newspaper upright."

He quickly turned the paper upside down and realized she was holding pancakes.

"Thank you," he smiled. He started hogging his pancakes.

"At least brush your teeth."

"Doctors say morning saliva is good for the stomach."

"God," she turned to leave. "By the way, are you going to the college festival?"

"*Ooday?*" he said with a mouthful of food.

"Ooday?"

"No Ooday," he tried to repeat, "Ooday."

"Today? Yes, today. Tinku's mother told me about it."

Youvik was quiet.

"You and Tinku aren't on talking terms?" she asked from the kitchen.

Youvik got up as if in a rush. "I have to get ready else; I'll miss meeting my old friends."

"I asked something. It's okay if you want to ignore me."

"No, we are not friends anymore," he got up and rushed to get ready.

<>

Youvik was taken aback by the elegant décor as he walked into his college. It made him so happy he felt as though a large balloon was swelling inside him.

Old memories came flooding back as he met his former classmates.

"Tinku, Youvik, and I did everything but studying," said a friend laughing. "Where is he these days?"

"He went to Delhi," replied a girl. "Got a job offer there."

"Good for him," said Youvik smiling. "How are you, Jenny?"

"Much better now," she hugged him.

"Are you and Tinku not together anymore?" Asked Sam.

She beamed. "That's why I said, much better now."

Youvik smiled, "Look at that broken staircase that used to lead to the library."

"Our *adda* (hangout spot)," she smiled. "We all used to gang up there after bunking class."

"I wish I could say…." said Monty joining them. "*Dear Life! Statue!*"

"And I wish I could say…." said Lucky hugging him. "*Dear Life! Times Please!*"

They laughed and greeted each other.

Youvik suddenly stopped while passing the canteen. For a second, it seemed like his friends were calling out his name. He strolled across the room and reached a table.

He let his hand glide over the desk and sighed. "I wish I had a time machine."

"You found someone?" Jenny quipped.

"Here? In college?"

"In life."

Youvik understood and looked around. "Like whom?"

"Someone special?"

"No one," he smiled. "But much better now."

They both stood there in that minute of silence.

"You know," she added. "*The emptiness that fills in when once-a-beloved says, 'Who are you?' is unmatched.*"

"I know, but," Sam patted her. "*If someone breaks up, it's an opportunity to revamp yourself, this time better and stronger than before.*"

"I'll catch up with you guys later." Youvik went

towards the cafe.

"He didn't even greet me." Sam laughed.

"He is a little lost." She smiled.

"You pretend to be strong, but you too are lost." Sam looked into her eyes. "*Go solo; be it a trip, be it a search, with or for, yourself.*"

She nodded a yes and looked into emptiness.

Soon after, the whole college was filled with chattering crowds. Youvik and his friends marched through the door and entered the playground. He saw a huge poster that read - 'Ask Me Anything, with our celebrated author.'

He tried to push his way through the crowded hallway to catch a glimpse of the speaker, but it was all in vain.

"Did I make a mistake by coming here?" He thought to himself.

"*It's neither about the journey nor the destination, but the people you travel with.*" A girl said on speaker. "And I am happy that I took my journey of education with you all."

The audience broke into a loud hoot.

Jenny tapped Youvik's shoulder. "Her voice is sweet as honey. Isn't it?"

"How do you find the time to write every day?" A guy from the audience asked her.

"It is my occupation now. But when I was still an aspiring writer, I would make sure to dedicate some time out of my schedule every day."

"And what if you are swamped with office and personal stuff." Another girl from the audience asked.

"If you don't have time during the day to pursue or even think about your goals, I would suggest that you set the alarm five minutes before you wake up. It might seem trivial, but that time is enough for you to plan your targets. Once you have achieved this, the next move is to loop step 1; set another alarm five minutes before the current one." She explained.

Youvik found a vacant chair and sat down to listen to her, even though he couldn't see the stage.

She continued. "Keep looping the plan till you start getting up half an hour early than your previous routine. Half an hour daily is more than enough to plan and start working on your dreams."

A guy from the audience chuckled. "Why only five minutes daily? Why can't I just get up half an hour early instead?"

"Has anyone here done it so far?" She asked.

All laughed, nodding a no.

"The fault is not yours, but that of your subconscious mind. It loves to procrastinate and has the gnawing habit of saying, 'from tomorrow,' which never comes." She explained.

The audience seemed to agree.

"It takes less than a month to transform your life and make you independent," she added.

Youvik and Jenny listened to the entire session patiently. As the fest came to an end, the ground became empty.

As he was walking out with Jenny, they saw students giggling and having fun. One of them went on his knees and proposed to a girl with a red rose. Their contagious laughter reminded him of his day.

"Missing Monica?" Jenny asked.

Youvik tried to hold back his tears. The next moment they hugged, and Youvik sobbed, resting his head on her shoulder.

"*Smiley tears and teary smiles are priceless,*" Monty said, joining them with their friends. "Let's go."

They were at Monty's restaurant.

"Chopsticks' Chopsticks," giggled a friend.

Monty patted his neck, "*Khargosh* (Rabbit)."

The guy tried to hide his rabbit teeth.

"Guys! You will get your special meal shortly," Monty went into the kitchen.

In ten minutes, he came back with a sizzling platter.

"So when are you leaving for London?" Monty asked, serving them *kebabs*.

"Who?" Jenny asked.

Youvik replied. "Next weekend."

"*Bhai saab (Bro),*" said a friend waving a hi-five at Youvik, "*London ki goriyaan* (girls)."

"Oh wow," smiled Jenny.

All friends looked at her and chimed in chorus, "Ahem."

"What?" She was clueless, but then she realized what

they meant and tried to explain. "This 'wow' was not for the *Goriyaan* but for the opportunity to go to London. But what's that opportunity?"

"Project," Youvik replied, enjoying the *Kebab*.

<>

At night, lying on his bed, Youvik recalled his college days, especially his time with Monica.

At that moment, his mobile flashed, "Congratulations."

He smiled, thinking it's a message from Monica.

As he opened the message, his smile faded. It was from Jenny.

"Thanks," he texted back.

"I miss the old days," she wrote.

"Likewise."

"I too wish I had a time machine."

"Hmm."

"We both are sort of sailing in the same boat."

"Different boats," he thought for a while, "Probably the river is the same."

"Hmm. Good night."

"GN."Youvik typed and put his phone aside.

He pondered about the mail he had received earlier. "Is that special someone Jenny?"

**

13.

Rewind

Not time, but circumstances repeat...

◈

Not time, but circumstances repeat,
giving you another chance to relive.

--

It was two years since Youvik came to London.

His office projects kept him so busy that he was cut-off from his friends. He hardly had time to talk to his family. He could call only three or four times a week with his busy schedule.

<>

"Happy anniversary to me," Youvik raised his glass to toast himself. "The one who can be easily deceived. Hah." He added with a mocking tone.

He sat alone in his rented flat in London. Drowned in sorrows. He took another big swig from his glass and muttered, "Happy anniversary to a silly me."

"Monica!" He bellowed as he attempted to chug down his fifteenth bottle of wine.

It overflowed and drained down his chin.

Fat tears oozed out of the corners of his eyes. He rolled

over to the side and fell into a deep sleep as he snored in his own arms.

<>

"Bottoms up!" Monica cheered. Everyone raised their cups in the air and yelled, "Let's cut the cake."

"Oh wow!" She was impressed with the cake Youvik held in his hands.

"A toast to the beautiful couple who celebrate their fifth anniversary today," announced Tinku. He winked at Youvik and Monica. He hugged Monica and continued, "And a very Happy Birthday to my bestie."

She cut the cake, and the celebrations began.

"Birthday is just another day. It's our loved ones who make it special." She said as she bobbed a curtsy to everyone in the room.

"Be careful!" Youvik cautioned. He held her and said, "You are tipsy, baby."

"Drunk me; I am not trust," she laughed. "I am not tipsy; I am Monixy."

"Yo, baby. Just a little high," he pinched her cheeks. She tried to walk but fell on Bunty.

"Careful," said Bunty. *"Have rum, I mean have fun. Don't overdose. Cheers."*

Youvik looked around to see that his sparkling home had become a big mess, he shrugged. "Mom will kill me."

"Everybody on the dance floor!"Monica commanded and broke into a robotic dance routine.

Monty rolled his eyes, "*Irony, we want to dance like robots and want robots to dance like us.*"

"Crap," Monica lurched from wall to wall and sat next to Tinku. "How have you been bean-bag?"

"Bean-bag is hungry," he tittered. He patted the bean bag he was sitting on and said, "I want rice."

"Divided we fall together we rice (rise)," she chuckled.

Monica picked up the coleslaw and asked Tinku, "Who's the cousin of cabbage?"

"Lettuce," he replied proudly.

"Yeah," she held his arm, "Lettuce… go. Lettuce rice (rise), together."

Tinku was quick to shove her away.

"*Ye kya hota hai?* (What's this?)." Monica kicked him.

Tinku looked at her, "Bohot kuch hota hai, tum nahin samjhogi; Karamjali."

Everyone in the room laughed out loud.

"Huh," Monica flipped her hair, annoyed, and walked towards the kitchen.

Tinku picked up the tray and ran after her, shouting, "I'll get some more chicks."

"Sorry?" Jenny laughed.

"Sorry, the *tongue of slips*, I meant chips."

"Close the doors," Jenny winked. "Ice is running out."

There was another roar of laughter.

Youvik slumped against the couch. Jenny looked at him and giggled.

"So, where did you guys meet for the first time?" Jenny asked curiously.

"Tinku introduced us," Youvik looked around but was unable to find him. "Where is the boy?".

"Oh," Jenny looked around, "Where is your girl?"

"The boy took your girl," laughed Monty.

Monty realized that no one else laughed with him. They all stared at him while he laughed.

Sensing the awkwardness, Jenny peered at the empty icebox. "Break the ice, guys, but uh-uh, there's no more left."

Youvik quickly got up, "I'll fetch some."

"It's alright, Youvik." Jenny prompted.

"No worries, I'll get some," he headed to the kitchen.

A split second later, they heard a loud roar. They followed the sound to the kitchen. "Youvik, are you alright?"

They saw Youvik stand there. As though a tidal wave had passed over him. Jenny followed his gaze. Tinku and Monica stood in the kitchen, embarrassed.

"What happened?" Jenny shook Youvik.

"Ask them," said Youvik as he fought back his tears.

"I was just..," Tinku turned red. He stammered as he spoke. "I was just searching... she had a fishbone stuck in her…"

Jenny understood what had happened. She held Tinku by his collar and stared at him, disappointed. She let go of him and walked out.

Tinku ran after her, "Baby, let me try to explain."

"*With due respect, go to hell.*" She shouted and left.

The night had ended on a bitter note. Youvik was in a lot of pain. He had lost his best friend as well as his girlfriend. He tried to drown the pain with alcohol. He gulped down one bottle after another.

"Happy anniversary to me" "Happppppy anniversary to silly silly me," muttered Youvik as he crashed on his bed.

<>

Youvik muttered in his sleep, "Happy birth... day to me, sorry, sorry, anniversary to me. Happy anni… fer... fary.. shoo… mee."

After all these years, the pain of that night was still fresh in his memories. Like it was just yesterday. The day it all went down. That day, because of which, Youvik celebrated his anniversary every year all alone.

<>

"It was a dream," Youvik thought to himself, half-asleep. "In the morning, when I open my eyes, I'll still be friends with Tinku."

His phone rang. He woke up and found that it was his mother's call.

"YOU! Which caves are you living in these days?"

"Dude!" Youvik said with his face buried in his hands. "I am not feeling too good here; it's too lonely"

He wanted to share everything with her. Everything he had gone through. But he couldn't get himself to bother her.

"Kill the loneliness by being with yourself, all alone." She tried to console him. "Or take a some time off and come home."

"I'll try. How is your thesis going?"

"Not too bad."

"I wish time machines were real. I would go back in time and repair a few things." Youvik gazed out of the window.

"But my thesis might prove that time travel is not real," she chuckled.

"Ahem," Youvik smiled. "I'll just have to manage without a time machine, then."

"Not time, but circumstances repeat, giving you another chance to relive."

"Maybe, Ma."

<>

The next day he was busy with work. He was so busy that he couldn't even check his phone, which kept buzzing almost the entire day.

He got to them at night. He scrolled through the notifications. "Not this again," he exclaimed, looking at his email.

He checked the date. It was sent five days ago.

<>

Dear YOU,

I hope you are good and your journey of life is going great. I hope you are travelling on this journey without any baggage.

Certain thoughts, sometimes, get stuck in our mind like a hook; tagged to a bag full of past decisions and regrets. Clip them off before they drown you with them.

Are a few questions still haunting your mind and heart?

Jenny is around. Take out some time and meet her.

Yours truly,
YOU

<>

He walked into a cafe and found Jenny sitting at a table. She waved at him cheerfully.

"When did you move here?" Youvik asked.

"A week back," she replied. "I joined the company the

day before."

"Oh, that's cool," Youvik nodded. He felt gloomy and dejected but still asked her, "Why didn't you tell me sooner?"

"I thought you'd think that I was stalking you." She chuckled.

"Ha ha," he picked up his coffee. "Yeah, chasing me to London, all the way from India."

"Ha ha, if I were chasing you, I wouldn't have waited two long years to move here. The company I have joined provided an excellent opportunity for growth and you being here was the added bonus," winked Jenny.

"Point," Youvik said, distracted. "You know, I'd always wonder how Tinku would turn up whenever Monica and I met. Now I know."

"I have deleted that chapter of my life," sighed Jenny. "Sugar?"

Youvik shook his head, "One, brown only."

She tried to cheer him up, "Health-conscious. Ahem."

Youvik smiled blandly at her.

"So, how is life? It's been three years. Have you met anyone special?"

Youvik didn't respond.

"I'm sorry to say this, but you don't look like you're over it..."

"No," Youvik pretended. "It's not like that."

"Then how is it like?"

Youvik went off, "I just lose my senses when I think about them. I loved both of them very much. They have hurt me in the past, too. It took me years to get over that. I feel disgusted that I fell prey to their ploy again."

She patted his hand gingerly, "Who can understand better than me? You know, he used to go to her house and stay overnight."

"Erg," Youvik ground his teeth. "And she used to tell me that her cousin was coming over for a movie date. What the.."

Jenny was quiet.

"Sorry if I am being melodramatic."

"Shh! It happens. Sh!it happens." she consoled him. "Last week was the anniversary, right?"

Youvik nodded.

"Mine too, but see the difference between you and me."

"I am trying to get over it," he sighed.

"Move on as I did."

"I'll try. I think I need to stop having expectations from other people. I should rather focus on my life now."

<>

Youvik watched as the gloomy grey clouds passed over the moon. His mind raced back to the hideous episode. He heard a ting. It was his mailbox. As he read the mail, he felt his spirits lift a bit.

Yet, he felt an aching pain inside him. He felt joy and sadness, both at the same time. He knew what he had to do to feel better. He called up his mother.

"Dude, I love you." Youvik did not even give her a chance to talk.

"I love you too *Puttar*," she smiled. "Now my Yuvi baby, what do you want from Ma?"

Youvik became emotional and teary-eyed. "Nothing, Ma. I just wanted to tell you that you are my life."

"Aww, my baby, my *Babu*, my *Shona*; my Yuvi, my…" Riya smiled.

"Ma."

"Ha ha. Do you remember what your Dad says quite often?"

"No."

"Happiness and sadness are like a black and white trend. Neither one of them stays forever, nor goes on forever."

"Yeah," he nodded, wiping his tears.

She passed the phone to Neel and whispered, "Talk to him. He sounds homesick."

"You-hoo, how are you, my boy?"

"I love you too, Daddy."

"Ha-ha! Tell me something I don't know," he beamed. "I could never express this to your grandparents. I am glad that you are able to do it, Mr. Hashtag."

"I miss your stories Dad," Youvik sobbed.

"I want you to tell them to your kids one day."

"Sure, Daddy." Youvik wiped his tears. "Why don't you guys come over?"

"Sure we will, but first, tell me what is bothering

you?" Neel could always sense when he was upset.

"It's nothing Dad. Let it be."

"My boy, you should be bold and unstoppable. At times it's okay to fight back. Tough times bring out the best and worst in us. So, act wisely."

"I know Dad, but it's tough at times."

"Nothing is tough but your skull, so think out of the skull box and let the thoughts fly." Neel added.

"I know, Dad. I had a small argument with my boss, and it's no big deal." Youvik didn't want to sound too worried.

"Oh, that's fine, my boy. I would have been worried if you were not having any issues at work."

"Hmm. Thanks, Dad. How is your new telescope?"

"It's great. During the weekends, I watch the stars all night long."

"And weekdays?"

"Busy with home chores while your 'Dude' is busy with her thesis."

"Ha ha, I like it."

They continued to chat for another hour.

"It's time we went to bed *Puttar,*" he yawned.

Youvik got off the phone and threw himself onto his bed. He savoured the peacefulness and confidence that flooded his body. At that moment, he felt as if he could conquer the world.

**

14.

Baggage

Forgive all before you...

◈

Forgive all
before you sleep.
You'll be forgiven
before you get up.

--

Youvik found a quiet place in the office cafeteria to sit. He stared at his phone screen while contemplating his father's advice. He sighed and dialled a number.

"I knew you would call," Jenny blushed.

"Maybe I am ready now," he smiled.

"Great. Let's meet tomorrow evening then?"

"Okay," he smiled, "The same place?"

"No, I'll take you to a different cafe this time. It's near the London Bridge."

"Cool."

"I'll ping you the location," Jenny added. "After office, right?"

"Obviously, I have a nine to five marathon called rat-race."

"*Human-race needs to quit the rat-race.*" She chuckled.

"Haha. True that."

"Let's meet at six, then."

"Done."

<>

"Joe!" A lady shouted out from the serving counter of the cafe.

Joe collected the coffee from the counter. He was about to pull away the extra chair from the table where Jenny sat.

"Sorry, I need this chair," said Jenny. "I am waiting for someone."

"Oh, my apologies." Joe moved to another table to pull up a chair.

As he moved away, Jenny could see Youvik. She grinned from ear to ear. She got up and pulled him closer, hugged him, and ruffled his hair. "Good to see my old buddy Youvik."

"Sorry, got stuck in terrible traffic amid the downpour."

"Rain on a sunny day. It happens only in London."

"Yeah," he drew his breath. He felt conscious as he stood really close to her.

"Oh, sorry." She offered him a seat. "So, how was work today?"

"Pleasantly hectic."

"The same story." Jenny studied the menu. She was overwhelmed by the variety.

They chatted as they sipped their coffees and nibbled on quick bites.

"London Bridge looks awesome." She said with amazement as she looked at the bridge with her eyes wide open.

"Yeah, I want to visit it someday."

"What?" She was astonished. "You haven't been to the London Bridge?"

"Hah. Nope."

"Life is simple, as simple as Quant." She laughed. "What are you doing with yours?"

They ordered food and chatted a lot sharing old memories.

<>

Later, they took a stroll along with the river and sat there for some time.

"By the way, you seem happier," said Youvik in disbelief. "It's terrific to see you in such high spirits."

"I told you… I moved on. The closure is always nice."

"That's what I was hoping for," Youvik replied and got up, "Coffee?"

They searched a café and went there.

"I know you both are not on talking terms." Jenny picked up the menu. She knew exactly what made her lips curl like that.

"After what he did, I don't think I can ever forgive him," he grinned.

"Last love lives a long lost life."

"True that."

"But whatever he did to you is in the past, and what you still hold in your heart is ruining your present and future."

"Easier said than done," he sighed.

"Get this straight, Youvik. His actions aren't hurting you as much as your habit of over thinking the situation is. You are weighing all the things that you have done for him against his deeds. I know you helped him with his studies, lent him money, guided him through the process of self-discovery, and paid off his bills and rent. Only a true friend would do this and expect nothing in return," Jenny was candid.

She sensed Youvik was about to burst into tears.

"Look," she sighed. "Monica confessed to me. I know how it all started."

He looked at her in surprise.

"Yeah," she nodded. "At that time, you were deputed for out station project. She was going through a financial crisis and had only Tinku by her side. He helped her come out of the crisis stronger."

He stared into an empty void.

"*See the world from another perspective, and things would be simpler.*" She added.

"Is that a reasonable explanation to ditch someone?"

"I know," she patted his shoulder. "I am not asking you to patch up your differences, but to learn from it and move on. Don't deprive yourself of a friend or a loving partner in the future by over-thinking the bitter experiences you have gone through in the past. That's what I did too."

Youvik looked into the emptiness, silent.

The server approached them to take the order.

"Let go and learn to trust again," she added as she looked at the menu. "You can ask your friends or partner to have some patience with you. If someone has broken your trust, that is on them. But you have a right to be happy."

"I'll come back later," the server said politely and left.

Jenny consoled him, "Carrying the baggage of thoughts for misdeeds done by others is like carrying a rotten tomato in your pocket for ages, the smell of which is ruining your mood and food for thoughts. Get rid of it and start afresh. Change your attire, wear a new YOU."

"People like Monica and Tinku are sane because they move on quickly. They live their lives in the present rather than carrying the painful emotional baggage of the past. They are opportunists who make the most out of life and stay happy, no matter what. We should indeed learn from them."

"Anyway, I would suggest there are more important things in life to concentrate on, like becoming a billionaire or travelling the world," Jenny concluded.

"You are right," Youvik nodded.

"Do Yoga or meditate on anything that will clear your head." She air-quoted - *"Nirvana; closing the eyes to see the world inside."*

"Tinku was 'Baggage' for both of us, which I got rid of, but you are still carrying that rotten tomato in your pocket."

"I agree with everything you've said," he confided. "Thank you for this. I actually needed it."

Soon, they ordered the food.

"Just so you know, they are not together," she grinned as she guzzled down her spaghetti and finger-chips.

Youvik shrugged and shovelled down his food as though he had not eaten for days.

"Forgive all before you sleep. You'll be forgiven before you get up." Jenny added, "My mom used to quote these words of *Prabhu Krishna* whenever I would hold grudges against someone."

<>

Youvik took the train back to his flat. He started outside at the clouds when his phone chimed.

"Text me when you reach." It was from Jenny.

He looked outside again.

"Tell yourself, to get lost, to find a new you." She sent another one.

"Okay, boss, and you too."Youvik smiled and replied. "Thanks for all the motivation." He continued to look outside.

His mobile flashed, "Jenny Calling..."

"Want to come with me for a play?" She quipped.

"Sorry? Play? Now?"

"O hello; I am talking about play; opera; drama."

"Oh, okay."

"What were you thinking?"

"Erm.. nothing. I'll check my meetings let you know by tomorrow?"

"Take your time. It's next month."

"Sure."

**

15.

Sustenance

The best company to be with is...

The best company
to be with is you
your-self.

--

Weeks passed by, and Youvik got busier with his office work.

"Any updates?" Youvik's mobile flashed a text.

He smiled, grabbed his phone, and texted back. "Too busy to breathe. Year-end is approaching, have loads of work."

At night, when he was about to sleep, unsurprisingly, he got a notification for a mail from the same ID.

<>

Dear YOU,

I hope you are in excellent health. Just want to say one thing, don't miss the opera.

Yours truly,
YOU

<>

"This time; not without you," said the actor, dressed as a warrior.

The princess held his hand, and they hugged. The audience applauded their performance. After the show, Jenny made her way out, along with Youvik.

"Did you like it?" She asked.
"Yeah. It was a different experience."
"Let's go have dinner; I am hungry."
"Sure."
"One of my friends is also going to join us, along with his friend, a girl."
"Ohkhay."

<>

They settled in the restaurant and ordered the appetizers.

"My mom is after me for my marriage now," said Jenny as she munched her appetizers.
A guy from behind shouted, "Give her my number."
"Sam!" She looked up and smiled. "You are younger than me."
"Then stop growing," he chuckled. "Postpone two birthdays."
"Silly you." She got up and hugged him. "Where is your girlfriend?"

"I dumped her just now," he giggled. "As soon as I heard that your mom is searching for suitable prospects. And trust me; younger guys make a better family."

"Ha ha, funny," she patted his shoulder. "Meet my friend Youvik."

"Hey bro, I think I know you," he said with a hug.

"Not sure if we've met before," Youvik smiled, looking at Jenny.

Sam snapped his finger, "I was a junior to your juniors."

"Ah, I see." They took their seats.

"Your girlfriend?" Asked Jenny.

"We broke up," Sam winked.

"Come on. We have to order more."

"She is just a friend, not a girlfriend. Actually, my senior, which makes her your junior."

"God! Is she joining?"

"She came here for a short project. She is going back to India in two months."

"Is she joining us?" Jenny repeated.

"One sock can't house two feet. If it does, it's of no use." Sam smiled.

"How does that even make sense?" She shrugged.

"It means..." he chuckled. "She had some urgent work, so she ditched me."

"Good. Anyway, what will you have?"

"Anything that moves." He scrolled through the menu. "Get something for your friend here too. He looks as though he is not eating properly nowadays."

Youvik looked at Jenny in surprise.

"Ignore him." Jenny chuckled. "He is too upfront for his own good."

"No, I am serious," Sam added, "Back in school, you were handsome and used to hone an athletic-looking body. Girls in my class would talk about you. And now look at you, man."

"Is that so?" Jenny smiled.

"Yeah, and the one who was about to join us today, she was one of your fans too."

"Ahem," Youvik smiled. "Corporate life did this to me. Not my fault."

"Sorry, but are you in a long-distance-breakup or something?" Sam quipped.

Youvik looked at Jenny. "No."

"You didn't even talk to me properly during our last college meet."

"Sam," Jenny stared at him. "*The best company to be with is you your-self.*"

"Buy nitrogen balloons," Sam chuckled.

"Sorry?" Youvik asked, clueless.

"*In depression, buy gas balloons; they would make you feel lighter.*"

"*Kuch bhi* (crap)," she looked at Sam.

"Or how about this?" Sam chuckled. "*Do as gas balloons do while in depression, inhale helium of happiness and fly high.*"

"Do you mind if I kick your..." She fumed.

"Yo baby," he chuckled.

Jenny rolled her eyes. "Did you read any of the self-help books?"

"Actually, yes," Sam smiled. "*10 Golden Steps of Life.*"

"That's why too many quotes from Sam *Baba*," she finger-snapped. "But trust me, you don't know where to quote and unquote the quotes."

"I am still learning."

Youvik saw them fight and smiled, "I've heard of this book from someone else before, not able to recall whom from."

"Sorry, buddy, back to your topic." Sam nodded. "I know you are not a nutritionist. But at least do some basic research and modify your diet to give your body and mind the best."

"You're right." Youvik looked at him.

"*Bro,*" Sam added, "The human body, like computers, works on GIGO principle – garbage in, garbage out. The health of your body and mind depends on what you eat, drink and think."

"Some heartbreaks," Youvik sighed, "No office breaks. All of that."

"I see," Sam pointed, "Look at her, two breakups and still a happy, hot damsel."

"Two?" Youvik was surprised.

Jenny understood what he meant, "yeah, the second one was just a few minutes back." They laughed.

"Just eat and think right." Sam added. "No matter what the situation is."

Youvik nodded in agreement.

"You need no nutritionist or therapist. Just list the items you eat on a daily basis and check the nutrition values at the end of the week."

"Sure." Jenny picked up the burger. "I, too, need to keep a tab on my diet. But tell me honestly, did you recently do any of the Nutrition session conducted by the HR?"

Sam smirked, "Actually."

"I was wondering how you suddenly became so health conscious."

"Don't distract me," Sam added, "Step two is to analyze and alter your diet as per the chart."

"Right," Youvik picked up the menu, "Let me see what I can have."

"The best health resolution is not just attainment, but sustenance," Sam remarked.

"Hmm, okay. I'll start right away. No more burgers or carbonated drinks for me," Youvik winked.

"No worries," Jenny picked up his burger. "I'll finish it."

"A thousand dollars each," Sam winked.

"What for?" Jenny quipped.

"Oh, sorry," Sam winked, "Pounds; not dollars."

"For?"

"My consultancy fee."

"All we can offer you is a burger, so eat this, or else you won't even get that."

Youvik laughed, "Thanks for the diet plan, but I'll skip it for a month. My parents are coming over."

"Trust me," Sam laughed. "If your parents are coming, then you don't need any diet plan."

"Wow," Jenny seemed happy. "*Pranthe*."

Sam looked at her, "You'll turn into a potato one day."

"But you'll still love me, no?" She chuckled.

"You guys should come over on the weekend." Youvik smiled.

"*Le; eh vee koi puchan wali gall ae?* (Ah; it's a no-brainer?)." Sam gave him a hi-five.

**

16.

Deja

Trips have jet-lags and I-ll-miss-you...

◈

Trips have
jet-lags and
I-ll-miss-you tags;
but they have
long-time-no-see gags
as well.

--

Next day, Youvik was busy on his system at office.

"Is the deck ready, Youvik?" Asked his boss as he reached his desk.

"Hi Tom, not yet, post lunch" Youvik replied and looked at time, "Will send it to offshore for consolidation."

"Never mind, when you're ready."

<>

At lunch, Youvik sat with his team.

"Why does your offshore boss mark the whole world in the e-mails? What's his name?" Asked Liam, one of his colleagues.

"Parv?" Youvik shrugged. "No idea."

"You know he asked me to review your deck. He marked offshore bosses and asked me to send it to him for a final review before you send it to Tom."

Youvik was shocked. "This is really weird."

"Micro-managing bosses have micro-mini-mindsets." Chuckled Liam.

"True that."

"And trust me," Liam added. "He'll send it to Tom without marking me or you."

<>

At 4 pm, everyone settled in the conference room with their coffee mugs. The off-shore team joined them via video call.

The presentation began. Youvik was shocked to see his name replaced with Parv as the preparer of the deck. As he looked at Liam, he raised his brows whispering, "Told ya."

<>

A flight landed at the Heathrow airport. A man was excited as he got off the plane.

"Yay, *Fly-day,*"

"It's over now," said the lady smiling. "Did you text him?"

"Whom?"

She rolled her eyes and took out her phone. "Yeah, we

have reached. Okay."

Youvik stood at the exit terminal with a bouquet to greet them. He rushed to hug his parents. Tears slid down his cheeks as he hugged them tightly.

On their way home, Riya gave him something.

"*Kaju Katli*!" shouted Youvik, excited. He bit into three pieces at once, "Dude, I missed this a lot."

"It was a long stopover," Neel stretched his arms.

She murmured, reading a quote on exit point. "*Trips have jet-lags and I-ll-miss-you tags; but they have long-time-no-see gags as well.*"

"Good one," nodded Neel looking at the quote.

"Spot on," Youvik smiled and turned to his father. "How is your stargazing treating you dad?"

"All good. If I don't see stars, I spy on neighbours."

"Why did you spend on the flowers?" She quipped. "These are of no use after 2-3 days.

"Ma!" Youvik rolled his eyes, "It's okay."

Neel pulled out a flower and tugged it behind her ear, "Happy baby?"

On the way back home, she updated Youvik about everything from their relatives to her thesis. Neel, on his part, made his famous philosophical sermons about the world. They were never-ending. To top it off, Youvik talked about his passions; computers and physics.

<>

The next day, Youvik came back from the office

knocked the door.

His mother opened the door with a ladle in her hand.

"Dude! Am I experiencing *Deja Bhoo*?" He smiled looking at the ladle.

"Not sure," she laughed, "I can hit you with this to make you *pheel* it?"

"*Bery bery phunny*," he mimicked her.

"Your friend is here with her brother, and she told me the whole story."

"Sorry? Who?" Youvik was surprised. "And what story?"

"That you are making excuses not to marry her," replied Sàm.

Youvik laughed. He hung his coat behind the door. "Let's get married right away. Right now!"

"Sorry, we are busy with *Pranthas*." Jenny chuckled and took a bite off a huge, buttery *Prantha*.

"Oh, and what about your diet plan?"

"Next month," Sam winked. He licked his fingers and said, "For now *Pranthas* are a priority."

<>

Youvik freshened up and joined them. He hugged his father. "Dad, I have something for you."

He gave him an envelope. Neel opened the envelope and smiled widely. "Wow! Royal Observatory tickets."

"And what did you get for me?" Asked Riya. She carefully put down the pizza on the table.

"We'll buy you a solitaire from Oxford Street," said Youvik and winked at his father, "Using Dad's card."

"I am on a planned-sick-leave tomorrow," chuckled father. They all laughed.

"Wow," Jenny remarked. She looked at the pizza. "Pizza with *Rajmah* toppings! Your mom is really a dude."

Neel picked up a slice and licked the sauce. "*Nirvana*." All of them imitated him and laughed.

They all enjoyed the evening.

<>

The next day, they went to the Greenwich Observatory. Neel was in a happy high state throughout the trip.

They had a picnic lunch in the park, and after spending the day there, they went to central London for dinner.

"The Bridge looks so beautiful from here," Riya said as she gazed out of the window.

"Jenny brought me here the first time," said Youvik. He sipped his coffee.

"She is a nice girl."

"No."

"Is she not?"

"No, she is," Youvik looked at her. "But I know where you are coming from."

"We are coming from India," chuckled Neel.

"Dad has changed a lot," smiled Youvik. "Now he jokes more often."

"You are ignoring me," she said.

"Aww." Neel got up and kissed her. "My baby, I am not ignoring you."

"I am seeing another side of dad." Youvik laughed. "He is in London mode."

"Don't ask me how I handle him." Riya wiped her cheek. "Anyway, if you don't find someone, we'll find someone for you."

"Hmm." Youvik nodded. "I am looking for a wife, but thinking; whose wife."

"*Chaper paegi* (I'll smack you)," she chuckled.

"Ahh, you are getting violent, Dude." Youvik was surprised. "In London, you are not supposed to hit your kids. I can sue you, you know."

"Find a girl," she said with a gulp. "We get worried for you."

He noticed a tear peaked out from the corner of his mother's eyes. "Oho, mommy." He got up and hugged her.

Neel, too, got up and kissed her again. "Dare you to make my baby cry."

Youvik turned towards his father, and he kissed him, too. He asked the person who sat at the next table to click their picture. The father and son duo kissed Riya and posed.

After dinner, Neel looked at the sauce leftover on his plate and leaned towards the plate. He picked it up – that moment, Riya noticed what he was doing and took the plate from him.

<>

The next day, the family roamed around Oxford Street.

"There are so many beautiful women here, in London." Riya observed. "Don't you like anyone in your office?"

"Dude! Not here, please."

"Ok, let's go somewhere else."

"Ma."

Later they went to London Bridge. They walked on the glass floor on the bridge.

"So scary." Neel was nervous. He looked down through the glass floor at the river. "The height is making me weak in the knees."

"You are scared, not of heights, but of falling." Smirked Riya.

Youvik clicked a lot of pictures of them. As the bridge was opened for the ships to pass by all were mesmerised, so were his parents. In no time captured his parents' reaction.

<>

Later, they went to a restaurant for dinner.

"I am bored of eating at restaurants." Riya looked at

the menu and commented.

"Me too." Neel added. "I don't like the plates here."

"Plates?" Youvik laughed. "Okay, I'll cook for you guys next weekend."

"That's why I am asking you to get married."

"Ma, I'll marry a girl, not a cook."

"When did I say that she'll cook for you?" She chuckled. "You'll have someone to cook for."

"Gotcha." Youvik curled his lips.

"So, I have created a profile for you on a matrimonial website."

"That's so awkward, Ma." Youvik cribbed. "Parents finding their children's soul mate for them and that too in this era."

"Okay, then find someone on *Dinder*."

"Sorry." Youvik gulped. "Who told you about all this?"

"Mr. Jatinder told us about *Dinder*," chuckled Neel, and they all laughed.

"It's high time you settled down *Puttar*," she sighed, "Since we are here, we can help you."

"Okay, I'll search one soon."

"*Kha meri kasam.*"

"Not today please."

They had their dinner, strolled for some more time and then went back home.

**

17.

Irony

With great light comes...

◈

With great light
comes a big shadow.

--

Youvik looked at the mirror and styled his hair with some gel. "I can't believe you have already setup a meeting with them."

It was a weekend. Youvik and his parents were going out.

"At least show me a picture of hers," said Youvik. He was driving.

"As discussed." Riya air-quoted. "I had sent you the photo last Monday after our discussion."

"Oh, wow." Youvik too air-quoted. "I am so grateful to you for your kindness."

"*Puttar*," His father smiled, "Hold onto the steering. I want a peaceful death. I certainly don't want to die on the road."

His mother showed him his phone as he parked the car. He quickly looked at the girl's photo and blushed a little.

"You are welcome," she smiled.

"Ya," he laughed. "Thanks, Mommy."

<>

"We want the kids to be happy. That's all," said Riya.

Youvik and the girl's family sat in the living room. They chatted and exchanged thoughts about both families.

"Families are built on the foundation of love and happiness. We agree with you." The girl's mother replied, and her husband nodded with eagerness.

Later, the girl and her mother served the guests some snacks.

"*Samosa.*" Neel smiled.

"That too in London?"

The girl's father laughed. "Sir, every Indian dish is available here. People from other countries also prefix 'Indian' to the name of their restaurants here in India just to increase revenue."

"For the love of Indian food and culture." Neel picked up a *Samosa* and raised a toast.

"You guys can go and talk privately if you are comfortable." The girl's mother said as she offered the snacks to the young couple.

As all of them insisted, they went upstairs.

They were silent for some time. It was awkward. Youvik pulled out his mobile.

"This is my family, and these are my college friends." He said and showed her some photos of his extended family on his mobile.

The girl looked at a blurry old photo of Youvik with his friends, "*Irony; these days, images have so much noise, and people, silent.*"

"I know. It was our first camera, carbon-dated. We still have it." Youvik smiled as he gazed fondly at the photo. "This is Monty. We'd call him Chopstick. That's Tinku, Monica, and me."

"Typical Indian marriage system, you know," said the girl.

"Yeah," Youvik nodded. "Never thought I'd be doing this. But, anything for the love of parents."

"Same here," she nodded. "Did you have a girlfriend before?"

"Yeah," Youvik curled lips.

"Still in touch?"

"Nope. She left me years ago."

"Same here," she sighed.

"Oh, you too liked a girl?" Youvik laughed.

She was silent. Youvik's smiled faded. "Sorry, bad joke."

<>

Lunch was served. They filled the dining room with laughter. Youvik and the girl seemed to have liked each other.

"I'm happy that our values are still alive in this modern era." Riya said as she beamed at the family with admiration. "I would love to know the recipe for this *Rogan Josh*. This is by far the best lamb curry I have ever had!"

"Sure! Would you like some *Ras malai*?" Asked the girl's mother as they served dessert.

"Not for him, please," said Riya. "He is diabetic."

"No worries, would like to have anything else, *Bhai Saab* (brother)?"

"I'll have one more *Samosa*."

Everyone was busy talking amongst themselves when out of the blue, Neel began to lick his plate. Little did he notice that every head in the room had turned to look at him.

As he was done, he put the plate back on table, pulled tissue paper and wiped his chin; as if nothing abnormal happened.

Riya quickly broke the silence. "Anyway, you were telling me about the recipe... I am so glad you made this for us."

Gradually, they overcame the awkwardness. Youvik, however, still felt numb and stared blankly at everyone.

"We put curd in this." The girl's mother said with an air of superiority. "Also, we make sure not to use processed meats. You must be aware that it is as bad as cigarettes for health."

Towards the end of the evening, Riya gently whispered to the girl. "Don't mind him. He has contracted this syndrome lately. He tends to act like this at times."

The girl gave her a warm and understanding smile, "It's okay."

<>

On the way back, Youvik was quiet as he drove the car.

Half an hour had passed in silence. Neel leaned back with his head up, eyes closed.

Riya tried to lighten the mood. "Youvik. I was..."

"Shh!" Neel interrupted. He turned to face her. "Keep up with this silence."

"Why?" She asked as she whispered back touching his forehead to check temperature, "Are you okay?"

"My leg is sleeping."

"Youvik." She smiled. "Do you know what this numb leg situation is called?"

"Parenthesis," whispered Neel.

"Paresthesia." She corrected him.

Youvik was still silent as he parked the car.

Back home, Neel went straight to the bathroom. Youvik shouted at the top of his lungs. "Is this the way to behave in front of others?"

"Sorry *Puttar,*" said Riya.

Neel came back, took out his new telescope, and went to the balcony.

"I was deeply embarrassed," Youvik shouted. He rushed to his room and slamming the door behind.

<>

Youvik buried his face in his hands as he sat at the doctor's clinic.

"I cannot tell you exactly since when he has been behaving weirdly. One of my friends' sons, who is studying psychology, made me see the inevitable. At first, it was hard to believe. But, after going through the symptoms on the internet, I decided to visit you, doctor." Riya explained.

"With great light comes a big shadow." The doctor sighed."As we age, we tend to develop syndromes. The same is the case with him. I would suggest you seek regular counselling. It may take some time, but with regular therapy, he will be fine soon."

They turned to look at Neel through the glass window. He was seated in the adjoining room. He was bobbing his head.

<>

After they returned home in the evening, Riya lay down in the bed. She was visibly upset. Neel, seated on chair, massaged her tired knees.

Neel suddenly felt his tummy being squeezed from behind. He smiled.

"Sorry, Daddy," said Youvik. His voice quivered. "Sorry for everything I didn't do for you."

"I am not a heart patient, but *Puttar,* with the force with which you are hugging me, my heart would turn into a flat sheet." Neel chuckled.

Youvik smiled, wiped his tears and rested his head on his father's shoulder. Neel caressed his son's cheek with his right hand.

"Ouch." Youvik wiped his face. "It's the balm."

"It will heal your smile," smiled Neel.

Youvik applied the balm on his mother's knees. "I am sorry, Dude."

"Please get the doorknob fixed tomorrow. If you don't want peeping into your room when your that new girlfriend comes."

"Did it break?" Youvik was surprised.

"The force with which you shut it, of course, it did."

"Ok," he sighed. "Anyways, that new girlfriend sent me a rejection message."

"Oh." Riya hummed. "I have one more profile."

Youvik got up. "Let's call it a day. I am heating milk for myself. Do you guys also want some?"

"With a pinch of turmeric," Riya smiled.

The trio sat on the balcony as they watched the stars with the new telescope, sipping hot milk.

<>

The next weekend, Youvik took his parents to Madame Tussauds. Sam and Jenny also joined them. After that, they went to the London Eye.

"Does it snow here in London?" Riya asked as their cabin at the London Eye moved upward.

"Aunty Ji," Sam replied. "Go to Switzerland for the real snow."

"Yes, Aunty," Jenny nodded. "Two months from now, it will snow."

Youvik clicked their photos and captured the sunset.

"Our *fly-day* is next month," Neel added.

"Oh," Jenny pouted. "I wish you were staying here for some more time."

"We'll come back once you find a girl for Youvik." Riya smiled.

Youvik gave her a hard stare.

"I know a girl who is junior to Youvik's junior," Sam smiled. "Her name is Ni..."

Jenny interrupted him. "Don't confuse them."

Youvik gave him a stare.

Riya looked at him. "Ok, change the topic, please."

<>

The next month, Youvik's parents had left for India. Youvik was back to his busy schedule.

**

18.

Gone

Dear myself...

Dear myself!
Behave yourself.

--

One weekend, as Youvik watched a sci-fi movie at night, he received an e-mail. It was from his own e-mail ID.

Three years had passed since he received the last email. He was very relaxed, as the supposed well-wisher was silent for a long time.

"I really need to figure out the person behind these emails," he murmured. He clicked on the notification.

<>

Dear YOU,

Ask Dude to meet Mr. Singh's daughter for her thesis.

Yours truly,
YOU

<>

Youvik rang up his mother in a jiffy. He did not even give a second thought as to who might have sent the e-mail."Ma, how is your thesis going on?"

"Little slow," she sighed. "Sometimes, I get stuck with a few code glitches."

"You can take help from Mr. Singh's daughter."

"How do you know about her?"

"I just know. Anyway, you can try if you want."

"By the way, she too is a nice girl."

"Ma! I am not going to marry her. Bye."

"Love you too, baby," she chuckled.

<>

Youvik was in his office when his mother called up.

"Hi, Ma! How are you?" Youvik asked. He tapped his keyboard restlessly. "This isn't the best time to have a conversation, but I can spare a minute or two for you."

"*Puttar,* I have been missing you. Everything is good here. However, I do get tired easily. Probably because I'm growing old." She said in her usual calm demeanour.

"Tell me about it." He stopped typing and listened.

"Oh! It's nothing. My knee is good now, but there is a dull pain in my right arm for a few days now. I might go to a doctor." She said.

"Why did you guys have to leave for India in two months every time you visit me? Why couldn't you have stayed with me? I could have taken better care of you," He said furiously.

She smiled. "Only one-fourth of our life is left now, or even less. We get bored when you go to work. We have nothing to do other than Yoga, plus, all our friends are..."

Youvik interrupted and mimicked her, "... are in this town, and we have so many visitors during the day. We don't like any other city." He had heard it umpteen number of times.

"You know me so well, baby."

"Ma. Make sure you do visit a doctor. Don't work yourself up, please," he said. He looked at the notification he had just received on his phone.

Before his mother could reply, he interrupted her. "I'm on a tight schedule today. Let me video call you and Dad in the evening, okay?"

As he got back to his work, he got an e-mail notification.

"Bonus day?" He read the e-mail subject to himself.

Liam, who sat next to him, hummed. "I don't know how these personal data selling companies know what time our company declares our bonus."

"How much are we getting this time?" Youvik quipped.

"Peanuts," Liam chuckled.

That moment, another e-mail notification buzzed on his mobile. He did not pick up his phone but read the screen notification. "THIS IS AN URGENT MESSAGE."

He laughed. "After these companies know I have money in my bank account, I am VIP for them, and each of their messages is so-called URGENT."

"Read it, bro," Liam prompted. "It really can really be an urgent one and forward it to ten people else you will have a bad luck."

"Haha, good one," laughed Youvik, "I'll still read it."

Just as he was about to open the message, a roar of laughter from the next cubicle distracted him.

"Youvik," Tom shouted from the cabin, "Join us."

The whole evening was a celebration as Youvik enjoyed the bonus party with his team.

<>

The next day, Youvik woke up early. He killed time by going through his social medial notifications.

His phone rang and interrupted him. It was Tom, "Could you please come to the office ASAP?"

Youvik immediately got ready and called up Liam. "Project that went live yesterday has a bug in it."

Youvik went into a long rigmarole explaining the same.

Once Youvik reached the office, he got so caught up with deadlines that he did not notice his phone ring so many times.

"Argh, my head feels like it's gonna blast. I badly need

a coffee." He groaned. He and Liam headed to the cafe.

Youvik settled into a chair and leaned back. He took out his phone as he sipped his coffee. "Oh, God." He screamed. There were a bizarre number of missed calls from his father.

"Dad! All well?" He was worried.

"I have come out shopping with a friend and thought I'd buy you something."

"Dad!" Youvik snapped but controlled himself and whispered, "Is it that important? I have..."

Neel simply cut him off and went on. "I chanced upon this fancy gaming keyboard that's on sale. Should I buy it for you?"

"No, Dad. I don't have time for this anymore."

"But you work in a game development company."

"No, Dad, it's robotics and data science, not gaming. I'll call you later."

On his way back to his seat, Youvik scrolled through his inbox and came across an unread email.

It was the same one he had ignored yesterday. The one which read - "THIS IS AN URGENT MESSAGE."

He noticed that it was from his own e-mail ID. He decided to read it fully.

<>

Dear YOU,

You will regret it if you ignore this message.

Do not go to the office tomorrow. Ask Dad to stay at home at all costs. Visit your mother ASAP.

Yours truly,
YOU

<>

He started to sweat profusely. He immediately called up Riya.

"Ma, are you fine? Where are you? Is something bothering you? Did you visit the doctor?"

"Oh, God. YOU! What's wrong with you? You are bombarding me with so many questions. Yes, yes, I am doing fine," she answered, puzzled.

"Nothing, just like that. I'll do a video call in the evening." He hurriedly cut her call and called his father.

"Hi, Dad. When are you going home?"

"No idea."

"Mom had some pain in her left arm. Did she go to the doctor?"

"Is it? I think it was the right arm, and I had applied balm on that. She was fine."

Youvik sighed. "Can you please take her to the doctor today?"

"Sure, will do."

As he was about to disconnect, he heard his father

talk. "Yes, dad, tell me."

"Shall I buy you a gaming keyboard?"

He looked up for a second and replied. "Yes, Dad, I really need it. I work for a gaming company but they never gave me gaming keyboard. Please buy me one."

"Ok *Puttar*."

"Thanks, Dad. I love you."

Youvik came back to his seat and slogged through his work for hours.

Suddenly, he felt a slight tinge in his stomach.

"Uh-uh, I forgot to have my lunch today," he realized. He opened his tiffin at his desk.

Just then, he received an e-mail. Fearful that it would bear more scary news, he opened it with a heavy heart.

<>

Subject - URGENT!!

Dear Youvik

Don't let Mom read any of her emails today.

Yours truly,
Rev

<>

He was very sure that his mother was not sending him these e-mails. But he just could not fathom why the emails were related to her.

"And what the hell does this *Rev* stand for?" He wondered aloud, "Or may be who the hell?"

Liam looked at him. "Sorry, what?"

"Nothing," he nodded but couldn't wave it off. "What if Mom is indeed in some danger, or is this just another way to trick someone into forwarding unwanted e-mails."

His brain threw around numerous thoughts. "What's there in her e-mail that she should not be aware of."

Out of frustration, Youvik wrote back to the same email ID, that was his own email ID.

<>

Dear Idiot,

Could you please tell me who the hell you are?

And if you are pretending to be me, then I have only one thing to say to you, "*Dear myself! Behave yourself.*"

Yours Untruly,
YOU

<>

He pressed 'send' and waited nervously.

A moment later, a mail notification popped-up.

He quickly opened it and found that it was the same mail that he had just sent.

And he grinned. "Bloody same email ID. Obviously, I'll get it back."

He did not waste more time. He rang up his mother and continuously repeated in an undertone, "Dude, please be okay. Answer my call. Ma, please be okay. Answer my call."

However, she did not respond to his call. He quickly called up his father.

"Yes *Puttar*?"

"Mom is not answering my calls," he shrieked.

"Calm down Yuvi. I had a word with her just now. Anyway, I am going to reach home in half an hour. I will let you know. Okay? Bye." Replied Neel.

"Dad! Hold on! Don't let her read any of her emails. Dad! Daaaad!"

"Calm down. Why are you so nervous?"

"Sorry, Dad."

"It's okay, go on. I am all ears. I'm listening with four years now."

"Dad, don't let her read any emails."

"Okay, but why?"

"I'll tell you later. I hope you heard me."

"Roger that."

Feeling dazed, Youvik put his head down for a while. He increased the volume of his phone's ringtone. Ensuring it was no longer in vibration mode he started to work.

After half an hour, his phone's vibration caught his

attention. There were three missed calls from his father.

Youvik straightened up and called him back. He mumbled. "Why the hell vibration is still on?"

"How would I know my boy?" Replied Neel.

"Sorry, Dad, I was talking to myself."

"I have that syndrome, not you."

"Ha ha. No, Dad, you are perfectly fine."

"I know, tell that to my doctors. Anyway, talk to your mother."

"Dude, you okay? All well? How is your arm pain? Any nausea, headache?" Youvik shrieked all in one go.

"YOU, YOU, wait. Calm down. The way in which you are asking will certainly give me a mini-heart attack," she laughed. "All is okay? What happened?"

"Nothing, I just..."

"Seems like you had a bad dream."

"Indeed."

"Having daydreams? Are you sleeping in the office?"

"No, just, I... I don't know. Just take care of yourself."

"Yes, my boy."

"And don't read any e-mails today."

"Ha ha. What sort of instruction is that."

"I don't know, but just don't read any e-mails today."

"Oh, okay. I won't."

"Don't work on the computer today, and don't stress yourself."

"Gotcha," she laughed. "Call me once you reach home. Have to tell you something."

"Promise me."

"Copy-cat."

"It's copy-that, not copy cat."

"Roger that." She chuckled and looked at Neel.

"Khao Meri kasam."

"Ha ha. National food of India?"

"Yes."

"Ok; I promise."

"Okay, Ma. Love you. Bye."

"Bye *Puttar*."

"By the way, you can tell me even now."

"YOU; I said I'd tell you when you are home."

"Okay. Take care. Bye." He put the phone on the table and picked up again.

"Ma, you didn't disconnect."

"Sorry I was showing a photo of a girl to your Dad."

"I know which photo Ma. Okay Bye."

"Bye." She laughed.

"Love you Ma, Love you Dad."

"Bye *Puttar*." Parents replied together and laughed.

<>

Youvik relaxed and got back to work.

Tom came over. "Youvik, could you please be online after we file the submissions?"

"Sure," he nodded. "I can stretch today."

"No, no, no need to stretch," he smiled. "You can

login from home. It's just for backup. Leave at half-past."

"Sure. But half-past what?"

"Your usual time."

"Oh, got it."

<>

Youvik sat in the cafeteria as he talked to his team back in India. "See guys, he asked me to just login. No stretching is required. So you guys can leave half-past."

"Half-past what?" One of the team members quipped.

"Your usual time. Just login from home. No need to stretch."

"Okay and what about the signoff?"

Just then, he got another call. He tilted his phone to check and it flashed, "Dad calling..."

"Hey, listen. I'll call you back in some time. I am getting another call." He hung up without waiting for a reply.

He suddenly remembered the email and immediately called his father.

"Youvik!" Neel shrieked.

"Dad? All well?"

"Your Mom."

Youvik got up in shock. "What happened, dad?"

"She's no more." Neel broke down.

"What?" Youvik was in deep shock. "But I just spoke to her sometime back."

"Doctor said it was a heart attack."

"Where were you?" He was horror-struck.

"We were chatting, and out of the blue, she collapsed on the sofa." Neel was inconsolable. Tears were streaming down his cheeks.

"I am on my way. Be strong, Dad." Youvik grabbed his bag and rushed out without informing anyone.

<>

Seated on the plane, Youvik rang up Tom.

"Oh my God," Tom responded with despair. "I am so sorry about your loss."

"I couldn't signoff the working files."

"Don't worry about work. Take care of yourself and your family; stay strong."

"We are ready for take-off." The air hostess reached out to Youvik. "Could you please switch off your phone?"

"Could you please secure my laptop and belongings from my desk?"

"Don't worry about those. Take care, Youvik and; have a safe journey." Tom hung up.

<>

He looked out at the clouds. A wave of grief, coupled with guilt, engulfed him and ripped through his soul. He was depressed. He found it difficult to breathe.

"It can't be true, Ma. You cannot leave me." Youvik thought to himself. Tears flooded his eyes. "I had the gift of prophecy, and yet I could not save you."

"Are you fine, sir?" Inquired the airhostess.

"Yeah," Youvik wiped his tears.

"Do you want something, sir? Some water? Or something to eat?"

"Some water, please."

<>

Youvik reached home. They had laid down the body of his mother on the floor covered in white cloth. He knelt on the floor beside her. His breath came out in searing gasps. Neel hugged him tightly. Youvik struggled hard to console him.

"She hasn't gone!" Youvik yelled in disbelief. "She is just sleeping."

"Gather yourself, Yuvi." Neel's voice broke. "She has gone forever."

"NO!" Roared Youvik and held her hand, "Ma, don't leave me Ma. Please get up. Please don't do this."

Somewhere amid the delusion, his mind paused to think. He realized that his mother had never kept him waiting before. If she did not wake up, despite having yelled so much, the only possible explanation was that she really was gone. The relatives and friends consoled them both.

"We must perform the last rites, son." Youvik's uncle said as he hugged him. Every word caused him pain. Youvik struggled to keep it together. He sobbed throughout the cremation ritual.

As last rites were performed, relative and friends started going back. Youvik felt someone's hand rested on his shoulder. It was Mr. Singh. He couldn't control himself, he hugged him and cried his heart out.

Another elderly couple met Youvik and hugged him. "Be strong son, be strong in this tough time; for yourself and your father," the man hugged him. Youvik couldn't recall who they were but he cried inconsolably.

Mr. Singh hugged Neel. "She would always address me as *Veer Ji*. She was to me more than a younger sister. It pains my heart to see that she's no more, but we have no control over *Waheguru's* (Almighty) wishes."

Neel fought back tears and added, "She was so cheerful until the very last minute. Till just before she fell unconscious. I feel guilty that I couldn't do anything. I was sitting right next to her."

Youvik embraced him warmly. "It's okay, Dad. You had no control over what happened."

<>

"How did this happen all of a sudden?" Jenny and Sam were on the speakerphone.

"Doctors said it was a heart-attack," Youvik mumbled.

"*Bro,*" Sam consoled him. "Be strong."

"You know what I have experienced," Youvik blinked back his tears, "The biggest remorse in life is that when you couldn't say good bye, once, for the last time, to the one you loved the most."

"Be strong, especially for your Dad," Jenny added.

"I am not able to behave myself these days."

"*Bhai,* be brave. We may be miles apart, but let me know if you need any help."

**

19.

Flocking

Doesn't matter if the glass...

◈

Doesn't matter if the glass is half-empty or half-full;
what all matters is, that you have a glass and some water
and what you are planning to do with it.

--

<>

A month later

<>

Youvik sat in the passenger seat. Monty sat next to him and drove the car. They went to the market and bought two large-sized travel trolley bags.

They put the bags in the car. They were about to leave for home.

"How are you *Bhaiya Ji* (*Bro*)?" Someone shouted from behind them.

Youvik turned to see who it was.. It was the *Golgappa* vendor.

"Aunty *Ji* is not with you today?" He asked.

Monty looked at Youvik. He already had tears in his eyes.

Youvik just said. "One plate for me."

"Bhaiya ji, you no like eat Golgappa." The guy said while preparing one plate for him.

He took the *Golgappa* one by one and sobbed as he ate them. He recalled old memories of his mother.

Monty asked the vendor, *"Kitne huae* (How much)?"

"Wait," Youvik reached for his pocket. He pulled out all the money he had in his wallet and gave it to the vendor.

"Bhaiya Ji?" The vendor looked at Youvik in shock. There were so many grand currency notes.

Youvik remembered his Mom's words and uttered feebly, "Mom asked you to buy chocolate for your kids."

On the way back, he cried continuously. He visited all the places he frequented with his mother, including *Guru Ji's Ashram*.

"She was so simple, yet her thoughts were mind-bending." Guru Ji said. Youvik and Monty sat in front of him. "May *Prabhu* (God) bless the departed soul."

<>

Youvik entered the house with the two trolley bags. Neel approached him. "When is your flight scheduled?"

"Not mine."

Neel looked at him, his eyebrows arched.

"Ours," he said. He opened the bags. "Tell me what stuff you want me to pack."

"But..."

"No ifs and buts. I am not leaving you alone, Dad. You are moving in with me."

Neel had to give in.

<>

They looked at the house for one last time. Then, with heavy hearts, they started for the airport.

"I can't believe it's been a month already. Though she is very far away, I can still feel her presence."Neel sobbed. Youvik consoled him, as he himself tried hard not to cry.

<>

The flight landed at Heathrow. Sam and Jenny were there to received them.

As they headed towards exit Neel looked at a quote banner on exit gate and murmured, *"Trips have jet-lags and I-ll-miss-you tags; but they have long-time-no-see gags as well."*

He had tears in his eyes,

"Dad," Youvik hugged him.

"All well?" Jenny asked.

"Mom had read this banner first time she and Dad had landed in UK." Neel whispered.

Sooner did they reach home, Sam had already arranged for their food.

"Uncle *Ji*," said Sam. "Please take some rest. You look tired."

"It's fine, Sam. We'll have some food first." Neel replied. They sat down to eat.

"When are you guys getting married?" Neel asked,

out of the blue. He looked at Jenny and Sam.

Jenny looked at Youvik. He quickly pulled a tissue paper to wipe off the food from his cheek. "They are like siblings."

Neel laughed out aloud continuously for long two minutes. Youvik became teary-eyed and emotional. When did his father last laugh? Sam got up and consoled Youvik. Youvik wiped his tears before his father could see them.

Neel controlled his laughter. "Your Mom had planned to tell you about a girl on the evening she left us."

"Oh! I never knew this."

"I forgot her name."

"It's ok. We'll find out."

Neel snapped his fingers. "Tinku."

"Tinku?" Youvik looked at Jenny with surprise. "Who, Tinku?"

"Do you remember Tinku? Your friend?"

"Yes, Dad." Youvik nodded, his eyes fixed on Jenny. "Why do you ask?"

"Before that, promise me that you will never leave me in the ICU during my last days," Neel added.

"Dad!" Youvik sat beside his father and hugged him. "How can you even think I would do something like that?"

"You know Tinku?"

"Yes, Dad, I know him. What happened to him?"

"He was after the girl that your Mom wanted to tell you about. He wanted to marry her. But she never showed any interest in him."

Jenny was feeling nervous listening to all this.

"He finally married some other girl and shifted with her to the metro city."

"Good for him."

"But it was not good for his parents."

"Why?"

"She took him away from his parents."

"That's bad," Youvik sighed.

"Yes. He left his dying father in the ICU; just for that girl."

"Got it," Youvik looked at him, "And you think I'll also do it to you?"

"No, you can't." Neel chuckled. "I will include a clause in my will. All my property will be donated to the temple if you do that."

All of them laughed except Jenny. She controlled her emotions and blinked back her tears remembering Tinku.

"Dad! Come, get some rest." Youvik helped him get up. "You are tired. We can talk tomorrow."

"Listen before I forget." Neel insisted. "Your Mom also wanted to tell you one more thing."

"Ok, tell me."

"You remember the old couple who came with Mr. Singh to your Mom's last rites?"

"Yes." Youvik nodded. "They hugged me, and I was wondering who they were."

"Mr. Singh had asked for your hand in marriage for their daughter."

Sam looked at Jenny. He could sense her nervousness.

"That was her last wish." Neel tried to hold back his tears.

"I can understand, Dad." Youvik hugged him.

They cleared the table and went to bed. Youvik had given him his medicines.

<>

The next day, Youvik came back from the office to find his father on the phone.

"Hi, Dad." He hugged his father and went to freshen up.

"They are inviting us home." Neel said as he hung up.

"Who?"

"Nia and her parents."

"Who is Nia?"

"The girl I was talking about."

"But Dad..."

"Your Mom had chosen her for you."

"Okay." Youvik nodded. "Are they here in London."

"Yes. On a long-term VISA; staying with her."

<>

"You remember when Youvik had put chewing gum in Nia's hair." A woman in her 50s said. Everyone in the room burst out laughing.

Youvik and Neel were at Nia's place.

"Mom." Nia held her hand. "It was in pre-school and we didn't even know each other."

"I barely remember anything." Youvik smiled sheepishly, "And then I shifted to a different school."

"Yeah. We were just kids when we met."

"Black and white; as if age and memories are flocking together; into deep space." Prompted Neel.

"Lovely." Nia's father smiled. "By the way, we recently started a science project on..."

"Oh, please." Nia's mother interrupted. "Let's have space and science discussion some other day. I am sure that Verma *Ji* has other important things to talk about."

"No, no. You can continue, sir," said Youvik. "He likes all these things."

Neel also made him comfortable. "Once upon a time, I wanted to be an astronaut, but...."

"But?" Nia's father quipped.

"But I failed the medical exam. They said that I would go color blind anytime in the future. So they did not let me join the course."

Youvik was shocked. "When did this happen?"

"After I completed my education."

"Did Mom know this?"

"Yup. Yet she married me." Neel blinked back his tears. "She said- I'd be the colours of your life."

"Dad." Youvik hugged Neel. "Hope you are not experiencing any such issue now."

"It happens sometimes." Neel wiped off his tears. "Everything turns black and white for me at times, and the next moment it goes back to normal."

"Why didn't you tell me about it?"

"Your Mom asked me not to." Neel smiled warmly. "Anyway, I have gotten used to it."

"We can see a doctor this week," Nia's father suggested.

"I am used to it." Neel told him.

"Now I know why you love these black and white quotes." Youvik smiled.

"You know." Neel glanced at Nia's father. "Even Atoms are black and white."

"Lovely." Nia's father smiled. "And do you know that if we take out space from all the atoms, the entire human race would fit in a sugar cube?"

"Your knowledge is mind-boggling." Neel said, awestruck.

Both the fathers laughed out loud while the others just looked at them.

"You guys must be getting bored," Nia's mother chuckled. "Go to the rooftop if you need privacy. He will now go on for another couple of hours."

Nia and Youvik looked at each other and went upstairs.

<>

They sat in silence for a while. Youvik initiated the conversation. He showed her the pictures of his friends and family on his phone.

"Nice photo." Nia pointed to a picture. "Old friends?"

"Yeah, old camera too, carbon-dated."

"Golden memories, though." She smiled.

"You don't have any questions for me? Don't you want to know anything about my past?" Youvik quipped.

"Doesn't matter to me. Past is past."

"Any questions about, say, a girl I loved before?"

"I had a boyfriend. He ditched me." She replied.

"Oh, sorry about that." Youvik nodded. "Love is a difficult question to answer."

"Love is the only question which has multiple answers, and the fact is, all are correct."

"True that," he looked at her with a smile. "But, you know, I feel I am going through a mid-life crisis, even though I am not at middle-aged. Especially after Mom passed away."

"I can understand, but you have to be strong. You also have to take care of your father."

"I know, but at times I feel like my life is like a question. What next… like… like a glass half empty or half full types, you know."

"See, I am no expert, but all I can say is that..." She sat next to him. "It doesn't matter if the glass is half-empty or half-full; what all matters is, that you have a glass and some water; and what you are planning to do with it."

At that moment, Youvik's eyes sparkled. He realized what he was going to do with his half-filled glass, called life.

They chatted for a long time. It seemed as though they liked each other.

<>

Later in the evening, they all sat down for dinner.

"I think both of them like each other," Nia's mother commented.

Youvik and Nia looked at each other and smiled, seemed as if they agreed to it. And almost immediately, it began to snow.

"YOU." Neel got up with excitement and walked to the window. "I think your Mom also has given her consent."

Youvik noticed that Neel was sad and happy at the same time. So he went and stood next to him. "Yes, Dad."

"Look," Neel pointed at the sky. "She is blessing you both from heaven and asking us to have some ice-cream."

Nia and her family smiled.

"Okay, uncle. Sit. I'll get some ice-cream for all of us." Nia said. She beckoned Youvik. "Would you mind helping me?"

They went to fetch the ice cream from the kitchen. Ten minutes later, they came out laughing with the ice cream. Then, they noticed there was pin-drop silence in the room. Soon, Youvik immediately realized what had gone wrong.

Neel was licking his plate. Youvik turned scarlet with embarrassment as his eyes met Nia's.

"Sorry I forgot to inform you about this. He has had

this syndrome for quite some time now." Youvik served the ice-cream. "His health is much better now. Counselling and family therapy have proved successful, but he is still not able to overcome this particular habit."

Nia looked at Youvik. Her parents looked at her for an explanation. There was an awkward silence in the room.

"Strange things have been happening in my life." Youvik broke the silence.

He looked at Neel, who was busy enjoying his ice-cream.

"I got a mail a few days back." He picked up a plate and served himself a scoop. "That mail reminded me of my old childhood memories... how I used to lick my plate after finishing my food. Instead of shouting at me, Dad would clap and appreciate me. Later he would calmly explain to me why I should not do that."

As Youvik finished eating, he licked his own plate. Nia and her parents watched him silently.

Youvik looked at Nia. "All I can say is that I can't promise he won't do this again, but I can promise you that I'll love your parents as much as I love mine."

<>

Youvik and Neel came back home.

"I am experiencing *Deja Bhoo,*" Youvik's own words echoed in his ears. He wanted to shout and cry, but he couldn't. He desperately wanted his Mother by his side.

But he knew he had to do it all alone.

He gave Neel his medicines.

"Why are you so quiet Yuvi?" Neel asked.

"Nothing Dad, tired a little."

"I am sorry *Puttar,* if I did anything wrong."

Youvik sat next to him, smiled and hugged him. He was fighting back his tears. "You didn't do anything wrong, Dad, and even if you ever do, it's fine, I'll still love you."

They watched a short astronaut movie together.

Later Youvik patted him to sleep.

<>

Many months later

<>

Neel and Youvik sat in an ancient church.

After some time, they walked on the greens outside.

"You know," said Neel. *"Mothers couldn't be everywhere, so they created God."*

Youvik looked at him. "True that."

"You know, the day she left us." Neel continued. "We were chatting over coffee, and right then, her mobile buzzed."

"Okay."

"At first, she did not care to see what it was. I happen

to glance at her mobile screen and told her that it was an email from her own email ID, she asked me to pass it over."

"What?" Youvik stopped walking, surprised. "You are telling me this after so long?"

"I forgot *Puttar*."

"I asked you not to let her read any email that day!"

"It was unintentional." Neel moaned.

"Oh God."

"She seemed so happy." Neel added. "I still remember her last words - *'Oh my God. It's possible. I have done it.'* When I asked her what it was, she asked me to read it myself. I went to my room to grab my glasses. When I returned, she was lying on the floor, motionless."

Youvik was deeply shocked. He wondered that his mother, too, had been receiving similar emails. "God. If only I could crack it," he let out his breath in frustration.

A girl came back with three coffee cups, "Just hold it for me, please."

She sipped her coffee, "In a nutshell, coffee is a good nut."

Seeing no response, she quipped, "All well?"

Neel took the coffee and went around the church for site-seeing. Youvik explained the whole situation to her, the emails he'd received, and everything Neel had just mentioned.

"I don't know what's going on," said Youvik scratching his neck.

<>

Later in the day, they had gone out for dinner.

"Has he slept?" The girl asked.

"Yup." Youvik nodded. "His medicines contain tranquilizers."

"This is a nice restaurant." She took off her jacket. "The London Bridge view never fails to mesmerize me."

Youvik got up and held his camera at an angle and set it to selfie-video mode.

She was surprised. "What are you up to?"

**

20.

Forever

Dance to the tune...

Dance to the tune;
known to none.

--

<>

An year later

<>

Youvik was buried in a pile of paperwork. He was scratching his neck.

"Want some coffee?" The girl asked.

"Yes, please." He adjusted his glasses.

"What are you so busy doing that you do not have time for your wife?" The girl nudged him.

"I am reading Mom's research work." He showed her some old papers. "Look!"

"Just tell me the crux of it. It's too long to read in one go."

"Do you remember the strange emails I used to receive?"

She nodded.

"Those were not spam mails. They were carefully written for me. Ever since Mom passed away, I have been following the instructions in those emails; even before that."

"You should be careful."

"I am. I feel these emails have been trying to help me. I won't be able to go through the guilt trip again." Youvik said. "Her research was about time travel."

He showed her the thesis paper. She was impressed.

"She was working on the thesis confidentially as a freelancer for some agency. They stopped paying her. They told her that her work was crap."

"How do you know?"

"I read their e-mails." he continued, "In Mom's inbox."

"According to her, a person can travel to the future. But it is impossible to travel to the past."

He used the coffee cup and an empty mug to explain her. It was the same analogy Riya had used to explain the concept to him.

"OMG, I have seen it only in sci-fi movies." She looked at him wide-eyed.

"Well, she wrote a program during her research days to send messages to one's past self. It'll be a big hit if it works. Just imagine a new dimension of time travel invented by my Mom."

Youvik could not believe what he just said that. He was proud that his mother, a typical homemaker, had achieved something which was least expected out of her and even scientists could not achieve by far.

"You sound exactly like your father. Now come, have your coffee and loosen up." She gave him a head massage.

<>

"Spaghetti, please," Jenny said. They were seated at a restaurant.

Youvik looked at the menu. "White sauce pasta, please."

"So." Jenny beamed. "Did you ever imagine that you'd get married to such a lovely lady?"

"Never." Youvik smiled. "All thanks to Sam."

"I will always be there for you, my boy." Sam pulled up a chair and joined them.

"Always late." Jenny patted him.

"By the way," Sam added. "Instead of thanking me, you should thank her."

Youvik looked at her in surprise. "Why?"

Jenny smiled, "I talked to Nia about you."

Youvik looked at Nia, who was seated next to him. "Is that so, baby? Was she the culprit who got us married?"

Nia pinched him, "YOU."

Everyone laughed.

"I mean…" Youvik was speechless. He knew Jenny had a soft corner for him.

"I know she has a soft corner for you." Nia looked at Jenny. "Even after my parents and I visited your home, I had my doubts. After all, it's an arranged marriage."

She looked at Jenny. "Then, one day, Jenny

approached me."

"But." Youvik was surprised. "How did she contact you without going through me?"

Sam smiled. "Remember, someone was supposed to join us when we meet for the first time in the UK? It was Nia."

"Oh, what a small world!" Laughed Youvik.

"Friends, not yet met, the world is full of." Sam chuckled.

Nia looked at Youvik, "Jenny told me she had feelings for you. But since your Mom had selected me, she didn't want to get in the way of her choice. She told me everything about you."

"And all my affairs?" Youvik chuckled.

"Yes." Jenny giggled.

"I was after Nia," added Sam. "But anything for my brother."

"Oh, God!" Nia laughed. "It's not a love triangle, but it sure is a complicated quadrangle."

"But you never told me this." Youvik looked at Nia.

"I had asked her not to." prompted Jenny.

"I owe you both a lot." Youvik looked at Sam and Jenny.

"Expectations hurt, be it sorry, be it thank you." Jenny air-quoted.

"Don't make me cry." Sam pierced a piece of pasta with his fork. "I am hungry."

"No, I am seriously grateful to you guys." Youvik smiled, "You guys never fail to cheer me up and take care of my Dad. I sometimes don't miss my relatives and friends here."

<>

Youvik and Nia reached home. They checked on Neel and found him asleep.

Youvik put a popcorn bag in the microwave and connected his mobile to the TV.

"What are you up to?" Nia asked.

He took the popcorn bag from the microwave and picked her up in his arms.

"Ouch." She rubbed her arm. "The steam from the pouch."

He carried her to the sofa, sat next to her, and pulled a blanket over both of them. "Click the play button."

"How many times would you watch this?" She laughed.

"Shh! It's my favourite movie."

The video recording began. The screen was initially blank, but the background chit-chat was clearly audible.

"This is a nice restaurant." It was a girl's voice. "The London Bridge view never fails to mesmerize me."

The camera seemed to move slightly. It was being adjusted at an angle to take a selfie. Youvik's face was visible.

"What are you up to?" Asked the girl.

As Youvik moved away from the camera, Nia's face became visible.

"Your glow is making the restaurant shine." Youvik, in the video, had come straight to the point. "Especially in this gorgeous red gown."

Nia blushed. She looked around and pretended to ignore him.

"Speed of love is measured in blushes per hour." He looked straight into her eyes.

"Sorry?" She looked at him.

"Can I say something?"

"No." She laughed.

"Okay, thanks. I will."

She blushed even more uncontrollably.

"I met you; I met me, love."

"Can you please elaborate?" She smirked.

Youvik got up and took a step towards the central red fountain. He stumbled and fell to the ground.

"Oops." She got up to give him a hand.

Next moment Youvik went on his knees and opened a small box. "Lifetime, would you like to annoy me for?"

She was shocked. "What?"

"Quick. It's too cold, and my knee hurts."

"Are you serious?"

"No. I am just joking."

"YOU." She hit him on his shoulder playfully and extended her arm. Youvik slipped the ring onto her finger.

People at the restaurant cheered.

"Someone said..." Youvik got up and spread his arms

wide open. "Hug as if it is your first; kiss as if it's your last."

She embraced him and whispered, "Dance to the tune; known to none."

And they danced to the rhythm of their own happiness and soon were into each other, lost.

That moment, it started snowing.

**

21.

Byself

What if your younger-self...

◈

What if
your younger-self
could meet you?

--

<>

Months later

<>

"How long are you gonna take, honey?" Youvik was outside the bathroom. He was restless.

Nia did not answer. He was worried as she was in there for quite some time now. "Are you fine?"

"Youvik!" Nia shrieked as she came out. She ran towards him, hugged him tightly and cried.

"What's wrong, Nia?" He started to panic.

"Nothing's wrong." She smiled.

"Then why are you crying?"

"These are happy tears."

"For?" He was surprised.

"What if you could meet your younger-self?"

"Sorry it's getting tough, I am bad at guessing."

"*Mr. Daddy.*" She stressed the last word until Youvik

realized what had happened. She showed her the test strip. He immediately turned to look, there were two red lines.

His face lit up with instant joy. "OH MY GOD! Are you serious? We are pregnant? Oh my God! We are pregnant. I am gonna become a Daddy. I am gonna become a DADDY." He sang. "Let's break this news to mom and dad."

"Mom?" She rolled her eyes. "Right, we'll email her about our kid's arrival."

"I can make a program for that." Youvik looked up.

"Actually, you can send emails only to yourself." He explained.

Nia blatantly ignored him and headed towards Neel's room. "Let us share the good news with Dad."

<>

They waited for their turn for the sonogram. "I am thinking of quitting my job," Nia said.

"I would suggest you take a break for now. Don't quit altogether. Your career is equally important, Nia." Youvik suggested. "I know how it feels. Mom always wanted to get back to work. I'll never let you settle for anything less."

Nia smiled at him with awe. "Now I understand why Jenny admires you. She told me that marrying you would be the best decision of my life."

<>

<>

2 years later

<>

Youvik was busy at work. His phone buzzed. "Come home soon, honey. I don't want to miss the flight, like last time, and spend vacations at home" It was a text from Nia.

He immediately wrapped up his work and left for home.

"I have packed all our stuff. We are good to go." Nia bobbed a curtsy to him.

As they had settled down on the plane Youvik exclaimed, "You know what...."

Nia cut him off, "Shh, don't scream. You might wake him up." Nia jerking her head towards the toddler that slept in her lap.

"Oops. Sorry, sorry," Youvik whispered. "You know, it was me who has been reaching out to myself all these years."

"Is it?"

"It was *Byself*."

"*Byself*?" She was confused. "What's that?"

"*Byself* means By-myself."

"Oh." She whispered back. "How do you know?"

"It's urban slang, the latest one. Gen-x, you know."

"Ugh, not the word." She rolled her eyes. "About you e-mailing yourself."

"I am quite sure about this. My future self had been warning my younger self all along."

"Okay. So, are you saying that your future self can

message your younger self?"

A young man who sat in the row before theirs turned to face them. "*Bro,* I can tell you are drunk. Please sleep and let us be in peace." He said crossly.

"Sorry, but..."

Nia held his hand. "You do not have to explain to *him.* I believe you."

Youvik smiled and looked at his father, "Umm. I will tell him once he wakes up."

Youvik plonked himself on the seat. "Trust me. I have never been this excited for a trip like ever, that feeling of the happy family."

"It's neither about the journey nor the destination, but the people you travel with." She prompted.

"I have heard these lines somewhere before." Youvik thought for a while. "Anyway, this is one of the best days of my life."

<>

As soon as they reached the hotel, Nia fed the baby. Youvik strolled across the room and opened the glass doors to allow some fresh air inside. The balcony offered a beautiful view of the pool.

As Youvik freshened up, he heard a roar of laughter. He couldn't resist. He peeped into the living room. He saw Nia and Neel lick the ice cream off their plates. The baby imitated them. He stuck out his tongue.

"I feel left out." Youvik snorted.

"Give yourself a break and join us." Nia chortled.

Youvik unzipped his bag and took out a neatly wrapped gift. He pushed it towards Neel. Neel stared at him in amazement. Nia nudged him and asked to unwrap the present. Neel grinned from ear to ear as he unwrapped the gift. He was holding his dreams in his hands- a powerful star gazer.

"I'll search the sky and tell you guys which star is your Mom." Neel smiled warmly.

**

22.

Time-stamp

The start and past paths, can't...

◈

The start and past paths, can't be changed; but the future, certainly, with the journey to a great the end.

--

<>

5 years later

<>

Neel searched for something in his drawer.

"Dad!" Youvik came into Neel's room. "What are you looking for?"

"Screwdriver." He shuffled through the stuff in his drawer.

He looked at the telescope. It was lying on the ground. The stand was broken. "Any idea about the password for Mom's computer?" Youvik asked.

Neel sat on the bed with the screwdriver and the broken stand.

"Dad! Password?"

Getting no answer, Youvik helped him fix the stand for half an hour and put the telescope back in its place. "Happy?" Youvik asked.

Neel bent down and looked through the telescope,

and smiled. "Yes."

"Cool." Youvik patted him. "Now, any idea about password, please?"

He noticed that his father struggled to recall the password. He walked towards the door. "Let me know when you remember it."

"Listen..." Neel said and paused to think.

Youvik looked at him wide-eyed, "I knew it, Dad. Tell me."

"Umm..." Neel frowned at him. "Sorry, I forgot your name."

Youvik's hopes were quashed.

"Youvik." Neel said. He remembered his name.

"Hmm, why don't you ask your Mom, Youvik." Neel smiled.

Youvik scratched his head and patted his shoulder. "Good idea. Thanks, Daddy."

<>

"Any luck?" Nia asked Youvik.

"He doesn't even remember my name or the fact that Mom is no more," Youvik said gravely. He stared at the table lamp in disbelief.

"*Bro!*" A young kid shouted as he came into the room and stood next to her.

She held her hand, "How many times have I told you I am not your *Bro*, so don't call me *Bro*."

"Ok *Bro*."

She gave him a grave look.

"Where is my gaming keyboard, *bro*?" he repeated.

"Revik!"

"Sorry *Bro*," he whispered, "Where is my gaming keyboard, Ma."

"Who used it the last time?"

"Daddy."

"Then? Ask daddy."

Youvik jolted and looked at her.

"What?"

"Ask Daddy!" He repeated.

"Yes," she nodded. "You used it last time, right."

"Ask Daddy!" Youvik gasped.

"Of course. Now don't say you didn't use it."

Youvik shook her by the shoulders. "ASK DADDY!"

"Obviously." She was still confused.

"Yes." Youvik ran towards the desktop. He screamed. "Ask DADDY."

"What happened?" Nia shouted as she ran after him.

Revik too followed him. "Daddy."

Shivers ran down Youvik's spine as he typed ASK DADDY. He pressed the enter key. Logged in successfully. "ASK DADDY. Yes." He shouted with his arms wide open.

"Mommy." Revik began to cry.

She picked the kid up and looked at Youvik furiously.

"I have got in." Youvik smiled.

Over the next few minutes, he explained the concept his mother used to set the password and her coding files that were in the system.

He located the programme she had developed and searched the folders. In the mean while, Nia found the gaming keyboard and gave it to Revik.

"I found it," Youvik shouted.

"What's that?" Nia pointed at the screen.

"The source code from the backend."

She looked at him, confused. "But it seems to be in different language. If I am not wrong, it's Sanskrit. Right?"

"Yes."

"Then you will have to decode Sanskrit first."

"I used to get full-on full marks in Sanskrit in school." He smirked.

"Mom must have taught you that subject."

"Indeed." He giggled. "But I'll do my best to crack this script and bring it to life."

"Yes, make her proud."

<>

Over dinner, Youvik told Nia everything he had discovered.

"I am so tired. It feels good to unearth Mom's work. I miss her a lot today."

"She must be glad wherever she is today." Nia smiled and served.

"*Rajmah* on Pizza?" Youvik looked at her.

"Yaeee." Revik smiled. "I like it."

Neel gave the kid a hi-five.

"I know, Ma used to cook this for you, and you liked it a lot," Nia smirked.

"How do you know?"

"Secret sources," she winked.

"You know, Ma always told me that I should define my life's purpose in one word. It can keep changing, but I should always hold on to it somewhere in my mind," Youvik smiled as he reminisced.

"So, what is it?"

"When I was studying the script and code today, I discovered something, a keyword of the puzzle." He told her excitedly.

"What is it?" Nia gaped.

"Time."

"Okay." She nodded, "Go on."

"The timestamp of past dates is usually treated as spam if we received them from someone else's email ID, but…."

"Ahem."

"If one's own email ID has been used, and it is a future date, then there are chances of mailing your past-self. This is probably why I have been receiving emails from my own ID."

"So, mystery solved?"

"Not yet," he sighed. "I have just unravelled the concept. I miss Mom a lot but this way I think I am spending my time with her."

"You miss *Dadi* (Grandmother) so much?" Asked Revik. He munched on the pizza.

Youvik smiled, "A lot."

"Is it difficult without her?"

"Yup," Youvik sighed.

"The start and past paths, can't be changed; but the future,

certainly, with the journey to a great the end." Nia caressed Revik's hair, "Cherishing past and creating beautiful memories is what life all about."

"True that," Revik looked at her. "Tell me one thing."

"Yup," she nodded.

"Is a family possible without a mother?"

"Umm." She looked at Youvik.

Youvik looked at her, then at Neel and nodded. "Difficult, but yes."

"No," Nia added. "I think he is asking about something else."

"Ya, actually." Revik smiled lopsidedly. "I meant is a family possible if there is no mother?"

"Umm." Youvik flickered his eyes. He fumbled to think of an answer. He looked at Nia. "What is family?"

Nia understood why he hesitated and added, "A family consists of a mother, a father, a kid. But that's the old definition. A family these days may have one father or two and a kid, one mother or two and a kid, one grandparent or two and a kid, and so on. And sometimes a kid may or may not be there, and it would still be called a family."

"*Gotcha,*" Revik nodded.

Youvik laughed. "You know, your grandma used to use that word to tease me."

Ignoring all of them; Neel had last bite and looked at Revik, "This *Rajmah* pizza is awesome. When I will meet your *Dadi*; I'll tell her how much you liked it."

**

23.

Dreams

Give it a try, for you are...

Give it a try, for you are born to fly high;
don't sit on the shores, don't wait and sigh.

--

<>

5 years later

<>

"He hasn't returned yet. Can you look for him? He was supposed to be back an hour ago." Nia looked at the clock anxiously.

Youvik, as always, was buried in a pile of paperwork. His obsession with the mystery had grown with time. He was busy with printouts of the script. He found it difficult to understand the program that Riya had encoded.

Over the years, he had hired numerous freelancers and organized multiple competitions. He hoped that someone would solve the mystery. But it was all in vain.

"Hey! Are you even listening to me? This is regarding your son's future!" Nia snatched the paper from his hand.

Youvik moaned. "Yes, yes. Teenagers are difficult to deal with. I remember being one, too. Poor Ma, don't know how she tolerated me."

"What was I saying?" She glowered.

"Sorry, can you please repeat it?"

"Rio stole the pen from Revik's bag. And Revik yelled at him." Nia repeated.

"The classic teen angst, he will be okay." He patted her on the shoulder.

"He should be taught that one shouldn't hold petty grudges."

Youvik smiled sheepishly. "Give me my papers back, please. Otherwise, I'll hold a grudge against you."

"I will not repeat this again. We have a kid, and he isn't home yet. Can you look for him? He was supposed to be back an hour ago."

"Oh...we have a kid?" Youvik chuckled. She threw the paper at him.

"Mommy." Revik coughed. "I am hungry."

"Where were you all this time?" Youvik asked softly.

Nia stared at him for being so polite.

"Where were you?" Youvik frowned dramatically. "Tell me now."

"I was at Rio's place."

"Why?" She was shocked, "What did you do to him?"

"Teachers told Rio's parents that he stolen my pen. So I went to tell his parents that I forgive him and said sorry for shouting at him."

"That's my tiger," Youvik applauded with his chin up.

"My baby!" She hugged him.

"*Bro,* his Mom told me so many things about you."

"Oh. Yeah, she knows many things about me. She's an

old friend."

"She said, your Mom was once a celebrity!" Revik imitated her. "Why did I not know this?"

"You were not born that time my boy," Youvik giggled.

"She said - Son, your mother, was a coveted speaker. There used to be an online video platform where she had thousands of followers."

Youvik stared at her in awe. "Is it?"

"She's right," Nia sighed. "I even wanted to participate in a cooking reality show. Ah! That vigour of youth."

"But I thought that your only passion was poetry." Revik was confused.

Nia sighed, "It was once upon a time. I always wanted to win cooking competitions."

"Oh." Quipped Revik.

"But before that," Youvik prompted. "You, Mr. Revik, You are going to explain your behaviour at school. So why did you shout at him?"

"You gave me that pen as a gift." Revik hung his head in shame. "It was very close to my heart."

"I agree. But promise me you won't be mean to anyone. I will gift you a new one."

"Sorry, Dad."

"Never hold grudges my boy." Youvik pulled him into a hug.

"Ok, Daddy."

"And don't think it's all settled. I have a story for you later." Youvik smiled.

"No. I want to know Mama's story today." Revik

pulled a cute face.

"Oh boy!" Youvik giggled. "You are going to enjoy this one. And you can boast about it at school."

"I will give you a little background," Youvik said. "She started her journey with elocution contests. She would narrate a poem in front of the audience, and the echo of applauds would make her feel euphoric." He looked at Nia to complete the rest of the story.

"*Caution - Poems are sweeter than chocolates.*" She chuckled. "But these poems were not mine. They were my mother's. I found them in your granny's diary."

"Mom always wanted to be a poet. She could not pursue it because of her responsibilities towards the family.

"Month after month, year after year, I narrated her poems in contests and grabbed every trophy. Not for too long, though. I had used up almost all the poems in her diary." She continued.

"Oh," Revik said with a sad expression on his face.

"My teacher, Mr. Singh, asked me to write something new. I asked my mother to help me out. But she was unable to rekindle her writing despite trying a lot." Nia sighed.

"When you are scared of doing something, close your eyes and imagine you are doing it for your parents. - These were my teacher's words." Nia smiled.

"But..." She looked at Youvik. "I realized I was bored of poem contests. My interests had shifted to cooking. I thought it was my passion. And I wanted to participate in a cooking contest and win."

Nia continued as Youvik and Revik listened with interest.. "My mother asked me to tell our English teacher, Mr. Singh the whole truth. I took Mr. Singh for a coffee and while looking at a cookery contest poster I told him everything about my dreams."

"Did someone ran into him while he was holding coffee?" Youvik asked.

"Yeah, some stupid fellow ran into him and coffee spilled on his shirt and my dress as well."

"Oh God, that was me."

"Seriously?" Nia was shocked.

"Yeah, ask Mr. Singh." Youvik laughed.

"Such a small world."

Revik looked at him, "That's how you met Daddy? Like a movie?"

"Nah," Youvik chuckled, "I was stupid to run home for something urgent."

"So boring." Revik sighed and looked at her, "Continue please."

"Ok. So I told Mr. Singh the truth of using poems of my Mom and then expressed that I want to pursue cooking. To my surprise, he didn't shout at me. Instead, he asked me to come up with something new for the next elocution contest. Your granny also suggested that I should give it a try."

"Mom used to say..." Nia looked into the emptiness. *"Give it a try... for you are born to fly high; don't sit on the shores, don't wait and sigh."*

"That marked the beginning of my career. I studied how great speeches were delivered. I explored words and punch lines to help enhance my speech delivery."

"They asked me to deliver my first political speech at the college elections."

"Wow," Revik exclaimed.

"And believe me, it did not go the way I expected. My topic was - *'Freedom of speech doesn't mean threatening the freedom of others.'* Another contestant chose the topic for me. They tweaked it to hurt the sentiments of a community."

"By the time I realized it, it was too late. It was one of the most embarrassing speeches of my life. I knew students clapped to boost my morale. But I later cried my heart out to my Mom."

"Awww." Revik lifted his eyebrow.

"Hmm," she said in an earnest undertone. "I was the living example of dreams to disaster story. Mom somehow accepted the fact that she couldn't push her dreams on me."

"I kept myself busy with studies. In my free time, I used to watch videos or help my mother in the kitchen. I had to avoid my friends and her friends as well for a while because they always asked me about the speech."

"Win thy dreams," Nia added. "Mr. Singh used to say that. I realized that I found a special kind of tranquillity in the kitchen. I would always cook something delicious when I felt stressed. And all my worries would disappear into thin air."

"And so cooking became your passion." Revik's eyes

lit up.

"I do wish," she sighed. "But alas, that was, however, temporary."

"Oh God. So, what is your actual passion?"

"Cooking was a temporary abode for my failures. I actually never thought of it as a passion. Then Mom took me to meet Mr. Singh again," she said, with lingering suspense. "He helped me find my passion through Mommy's example."

Youvik went into the bedroom. He unearthed a dusty book and gave it to Revik. "Read this, and we will tell you the rest of the story later."

"*Win thy dreams.* Wow. Nice title." He turned the first page and smiled. *"Dream? What is it? If you realize it, it's everything; if not, continue the slumber."*

"This was my first book. Mr. Singh motivated me to write it. Then, Mom motivated me to publish it. She made me an independent confident girl, she always said, *"Independence means... enjoying the freedom and empowering others, too, to let them do so."* Nia ran her hand through his hair.

Youvik looked at the mother-son duo and said, "Aww! I miss my mom today."

**

24.

Multiverses

Let the thoughts be like...

◈

Let the thoughts be
like the universe;
always expanding.

--

<>

5 years later

<>

"Breakfast is ready," Youvik announced. He stood near the dining table.

Nia came to the table. She had wrapped her wet hair in a towel. "Thank you, sir. Is Revik not yet up?"

"Breakfast is my duty. Revik is yours."

"I last saw him take out his cycle early in the morning. He must be at Rio's house." Youvik mumbled. He took a big bite out of his sandwich.

"I'll call them."

"Don't worry. He'll be back soon," Youvik told her.

"*Bro,* please bring me food in the storeroom," Revik said loudly.

Nia was relieved, "Oh God! This kid."

Youvik got up and went near the storeroom. He

stealthily peeped into the room. He saw that Revik was on the computer. Youvik was convinced that he was doing something fishy. He moved a little closer and gasped.

"Dad!" Revik took off his headphones. "You scared me."

Youvik was shocked to see that Revik was studying the code that he had been working on. "What are you doing?"

"Let the thoughts be like the universe; always expanding."

"Copy cat." Youvik winked.

"Ha ha. *Dadu's* (Grandpa's) words. I want to expand my thoughts, so I thought I'd find *Dadu* and *Dadi's* (Grandpa and grandma) old videos."

"That's okay, but this script?" Youvik sat next to him. "Are you able to read it?"

"Sort of," Revik sneered.

"Oh boy." Youvik pulled a chair. "You know, I have failed at this multiple times."

"I didn't know." Revik smiled. "Feels like *Deja Bhoo; in Dad's words.* As if I have heard about the problem elaborated in this script somewhere before."

"You think you can crack it?"

"Well, not me alone, but we can do it together." Revik nodded with a radiant smile.

"Yup; and let's make Dadi happy and Dadu feel proud in the skies," Youvik gave him a hi-five.

"Right, as Dadu always said - Black and white, the vacuum of cosmos vis-à-vis occupancy of skies."

"Oh nice! You really do remember all of his words."

Youvik got up. "Okay, then let's shift this computer to your room. But no misuse. Okay?"

"Of course, Dad." Revik yawned and stretched his arms upwards. He noticed that Nia stood near the door with his breakfast in her hand.

Youvik looked at Nia. "Seems like he heard our email and time-travel related conversations when you were carrying him for nine months."

"Like *Abhimanyu*?" Revik quipped. "Who learned *Chakravyuh* strategy in his mother's womb?"

"Lovely," Youvik was astonished. "Where did you learn all this from?"

"I heard this story when Mom was carrying me for nine months." He smiled.

"If you really want to do this, make sure you wake up early in the morning. I don't want you to miss your evening swimming classes." Nia added.

"It's anyway, so difficult to get up for school." Revik sulked a little.

"Can't blame you. Teens are notorious for wanting to stay up late and for not wanting to get up early." Youvik said plainly. "What you Gen-X say these days - been blah, done, blah."

"Been there, done that." Revik corrected.

"Yeah; that only. Just set your alarm five minutes early. That's it. And read. The next week, do this again. Soon, you will start waking up thirty minutes early."

"Why can't I just wake up thirty minutes before the usual time?" Revik shrugged.

"Well, you haven't ever done it before. Even for the

morning swimming lessons. Have you?"

"Okay, I'll do, but from tomorrow onwards; for today, I am starving," Revik said, took the plate from Nia and munched on the sandwiches.

<>

Later that night…

<>

Youvik switched on the table lamp and turned towards Nia who was busy typing on her laptop.

She waggled her eyebrows. "Are you sure you want to give him full access to the computer?"

"I used to be on it all the time. I turned out just fine." He shrugged.

"You are different, he is different, and I am different."

"We all are different, I know, and we have to be careful with his choices, dilemmas, questions, and answers to all of that."

"We do have to be careful." She held his hand.

Caressing her face, he smiled. "Don't worry. I'll keep a tab."

"Okay."

"Is it not yet complete?" He peeped into her laptop.

"Almost; doing final check before I send it to publishers," she mumbled as she typed on her laptop.

"This quote," Youvik tapped at the screen.

"Yeah, what about this one?"

"It's neither about the journey nor the destination, but

the people you travel with." Youvik read.

"Is it not good?"

"I have heard that somewhere before."

"You must have heard it from me only."

"No; before meeting you."

"Where?"

"Got it; in one of college guest sessions."

"Oh. I didn't know you attended my Author-Talk."

"What do you mean?"

"Ask-Me-Anything," Nia said as she put on her reading glasses, "That was my session."

"Oh God. Wait a minute. It was you?" Youvik said aloud, astonished. "That aspiring author talk event in our college?"

"Yes."

"O.M.G. It was you?" He screamed in disbelief.

"Shh! You'll wake him up."

He whispered. "Was it you?"

"Let me think." She stopped smiling. "Yes. It was me. Didn't you see me that day?"

"You know, I couldn't see the face of orator, I mean you," Youvik replied. "There were a thousand people around you."

"Strange, I too didn't see you."

"Yeah, but you see; there is something or someone who did my efforts to make us meet.

"Universe." She chuckled.

That moment, someone knocked on the door.

"Yes." Youvik assumed it was Revik. "Come in boy."

Nia stared Youvik and pinched him, "You woke him up."

As Revik came in, Nia asked him, "It's past your bedtime. What happened?"

"Someone shouted." He rubbed his eyes, "I got scared."

"Come my boy," As Nia tucked Revik in.

He cuddled her and asked, "Story time?"

Youvik caressed his head. "So sleeplessness is just an excuse."

Revik simpered and looked at Nia. "You always wanted to be a chef. What happened to that?"

"She became a motivational speaker." Youvik chuckled.

"But what about poetry, public speaking, and cooking?" Revik pulled the pillow closer.

"Yeah… none of that was my call." She continued, "People enjoyed the book I wrote. In no time, I started doing gigs. I didn't even realize I had this talent all along."

"*Bro*… I think I, too, have a talent like this. It's just waiting for me to discover it," Revik yawned.

She narrated her journey. It worked like magic, and he was out like a light.

"He has slept," Youvik whispered.

"Get him to his room," she whispered back.

"You know, even I thought you were a chef when we first met."

"Really? How did you know?"

"I had my sources," he winked.

"Stalker!" Nia rolled her eyes.

"Well, you remember when I first sent you a friend request?"

"No, I actually don't," she beamed. "You see, I used to get millions of requests."

"That's not the point," Youvik whispered. "The point is, the email from the future had asked me to send you one."

"What??" She looked at Youvik with her mouth wide open.

"Do you think the person who sent the email is the reason we ended up together?"

"No, but he is the reason for Revik being between us today," he winked and patted his son.

"Don't you wake him up." She thumped his head.

"And..." he rambled on. "I have a strong feeling it is none other than my future self. Maybe he wasn't fortunate enough to meet you. So he wanted his younger self to meet you."

"He even told me that I would meet 'someone special' at the fest. The day you delivered the speech. It is all adding up now."

Suddenly, his face lit up. Something struck him.

"Wait!" he exclaimed. "It means that if I do something different from what my future self did in his past, it won't change anything for him!"

Revik moaned in sleep.

"You're disturbing him," Nia said, signalled that they should go outside.

"So... I cannot change the past... only the future, and that too, only mine," he explained. He opened the balcony door quietly.

"If you prove this, it will prove the existence of multiple timelines, or say Multiverses."

"Yeah, a colourful dot in the black and white sky of fantasies of humankind."

"Black and white; the heaviest of vibrant and at the same time lightest of achromatic." She smiled looking at the sky.

"Copy cat! Dad used to say this."

"I am writing a story; including all of his quotes there."

"Well, get written permission or else he'll sue you."

"He only helped me creating the log of his quotes," she winked.

<>

They sat in front of Revik's computer the next morning.

"Dad!" Revik asked while he switched on the computer.

"Yup." Youvik entered the password.

"I don't like studying."

Youvik looked at him.

"What?"

"You know when I was of your age…" he started his same old words.

"I know," Revik mimicked him, "I used to study days and nights under the candle lights."

"Right, and I never had guts to tell your *Dadi* and

Dadu that I don't want to study."

"Dad but that was different time; today we have many options, coding, programming, gaming, apps. Many of my friends are already earning through video ads."

"Okay then, don't study. You too can start living your passion from tomorrow; start your video channel from today."

"But..."

"But what?"

"But..." Revik thought for a while, "But... I have yet to figure out my passion."

"Okay."

"Yeah. I also have a fear that if I didn't study then I will fail in the exams."

"Ok; then let's make a deal. Study till you figure out what your passion is. And once you are sure that you want to pursue your passion; you can drop-out from school or college."

"Done."

"Good, now let's start working on the code."

They started reading the code. Youvik helped Revik to understand a few of Sanskrit words.

"This program has no result command. Does it mean that the sender cannot access the results?" Revik asked.

Youvik took a sip of his coffee. "Unlike those two ticks and blue color in the common messaging apps."

"Hey! I never thought of comparing it to those chatting apps of this era. You are a genius." Youvik patted him.

They were busy with the code the whole day. Nia made sure they were well fed. She kept the food, snacks, and drinks coming.

<>

Later in the evening, they headed towards the dining table.

"Daddy," quipped Revik. "Any payout for the day?"

"I can narrate a story."

He thought for a while and nodded. "Okay."

"Okay then," Youvik sighed. "This story is about a teacher who was too old. He was out on an evening walk. A luxury sedan car suddenly stopped in front of him. A boy emerged from the car and walked towards him."

**

25.

Peace

Life be like, water...

◈

Life be like, water;
transparent yet necessary,
adjusting yet driving,
calm yet powerful.

--

"Who are you, son? Why are you touching my feet?" Asked the old man.

"Sir! I was your student. You used to tell me that I would end up becoming a mechanic if I didn't study well."

The teacher's face glowed. "Bunty? From the backbencher's gang?"

"Master *Ji*," the guy shook his head. "Do you remember the student who'd make caricatures of teachers, and you'd punish him even though he was a good student academically?"

"Sorry?" The teacher was confused.

"Sir, you always taught me that - *Being lucky is in your hands as it's the outcome of your deeds.*"

"Lucky?" The teacher screamed.

"Yes master ji." The guy hugged him. They chatted for a while about the old school days. After some time, another person joined them.

The teacher was quick to recognize him. "You must be Bunty, right?"

He nodded with a smile.

"Come on, give me a hug."

They greeted each other, and the three of them continued chatting.

"Sir, we'll take your leave now," Lucky said. "I stopped just to meet you. We are getting late for a meeting."

As they walked towards the car, the teacher was shocked to see Bunty put on a driver's hat. He murmured, "Silly boy, he could have been in Lucky's position had he been more passionate about studies."

<>

"Now, why did I tell you this story?" Youvik asked.

"I don't know," Revik shrugged. "Maybe you want me to study more and more?"

"No, the story is not over," Youvik smiled. "Here is the rest of it."

"Later that evening, Bunty was having tea with the teacher at his home.

"The teacher was astonished - I never knew you started a company of your own and now own a fleet of a hundred and fifty cars and drivers." Youvik narrated.

"So Bunty must be richer than Lucky?" Revik quipped.

"Everyone has their own definition of being rich; some are by money; some, by contentment."

"*Gotcha,*" he snapped his fingers. "Go on, please."

Youvik continued, "You may think that maybe the boy who grew up to be a driver enjoys being an entrepreneur. Success has different definitions for everyone."

"True," Revik looked thoughtful. "The driver was his own boss."

"So, there is much more to life than just studying; but for that, you have to have a passion."

"Right," Revik nodded.

"My teacher used to say..." Youvik added. "*Life be like, water; transparent yet necessary, adjusting yet driving, calm yet powerful.*"

"Nice one."

"Mr. Singh's story?" Asked Nia as she served the food.

"Maybe yes," Youvik giggled.

"*Bro,* include this in your next novel."

"Good idea," she said.

"Anyway, how far have you guys reached in de-coding?"

"Not too sure," Youvik sighed, "But I forgot to ask you, boy, how did you learn this much?"

"*Dadu* (Grandpa) used to motivate me to learn to code. I decided back then itself that one of my optional subjects will be computers."

"Hmm," Youvik nodded. "Let's work on it further tomorrow."

**

26.

Re-loop

Black and white, severally...

◈

Black and white, severally incomplete
and at the same time, completely several.

--

<>

2 years later

<>

Two years had passed and family continued their normal life day after another. Youvik and Revik so far had no luck to decode the programme; until one day…

"Dad," roared Revik. "I found this text in the email archive of this program."

Youvik leaned forward. He adjusted his spectacles. Nia also peeked in.

<>

The mail read -

Dear YOU,

I hope things are great with you. If you are reading

this, what I am about to say might come as a shock to you. I have plotted everything that has happened so far in your life. It has all gone according to my plan. One of the plans was to connect you with your all-time school crush, the junior of your junior.

I hope you got the love of your life. Marrying Nia would've been a dream come true for me. But I could never achieve it. I missed so many chances to meet her.

So I gave you pointers to meet her to attend her seminar at a college reunion. Asked you to meet Jenny, who had invited Sam, who was bringing Nia to the café. Connecting Mom to Mr. Singh's daughter, who was Nia's best friend.

I could never marry her, but no regrets; Jenny is a great wife, and we are blessed with a lovely daughter named Joy.

Yours Truly,
YOU

<>

Revik looked at Youvik, "How is this possible, Dad."

"How did you find this e-mail?" Asked Youvik.

"I searched the archive with your name, and all the e-mails got displayed. Then I searched it with my name and found nothing. Lastly, I found this with Mom's name."

Youvik scratched his neck. He looked at Nia. "I was right, you see."

"That's mind-bending." She nodded, blushing, "But tell me one thing. Did you like me so much?"

"Yes, I was right. If my future self changes his past, then another past is created in a parallel universe. In this parallel universe, I am married to you. In the other one, from where my future self is sending me e-mails, I am married to Jenny."

"No reply to my question." Nia sighed. "All men change after marriage."

"Right." Youvik snapped his finger.

"What?" She asked furiously.

"Not you." He turned to Revik. "Can you send a mail through this program?"

"To whom?"

"To me."

"Well, I can try; which back-date you want to send it to?"

"Put any random one," Youvik took the keyboard from him and entered the date but didn't know what to do next.

Then he looked at Revik. "Where do we enter the e-mail text."

"I'll have to encrypt it." Revik took the keyboard back. "Tell me what to write?"

Youvik narrated...

<>

Subject - URGENT!!

Dear Youvik,

Don't let Mom read any of her emails today.

Yours truly,
Youvik

<>

As Revik encrypted the code, he asked excitedly, "What is this mail about?"

"About your *Dadi.*" Youvik looked at Nia. "Dad told me she passed away that day after reading her email."

"Wait a second." Nia prompted. "Does it mean she had an attack because she was too excited to bear news in the e-mail?"

"Did she get an e-mail from her younger self?" Revik asked. "Maybe she was too excited that her younger self could crack the code?"

"Possibly." Youvik scratched his neck again. "It's giving me jitters."

"Calm down. Have a seat." Nia pushed the roller chair towards him and massaged his shoulders. "Relax."

"Wait." He rolled the chair towards the computer. "It means so far through this program, the elder self can talk to the younger self. But she was successful in communicating with her younger self. She told her younger-self to update the program and send a confirmation message to her elder-self."

"Seems like that," nodded Revik.

Youvik clapped. "Mom was a genius."

"Wait, wait." Nia looked at Youvik. "Take it slow, don't get too excited."

"I am okay," said Youvik got up. His left leg started shivering as he stumbled to walk.

"Youvik..." Nia leaned forward to support him.

"I am feeling a little giddy." Youvik opened the top button of his t-shirt.

"I'll get some water." Nia ran to the kitchen.

That moment she heard Revik roar. She threw the bottle in the sink and rushed back to the room and found Revik stood, hands on head. Youvik was seated in the chair, still and silent, he didn't blink.

"Youvik," she shouted and rushed towards him.

Youvik was silent. With his eyes wide open, he looked at the screen in shock.

"O God! You guys will give me a heart attack someday," she sat on her knees next to him and looked at the screen.

It was a mail that read -

<>

Dear Idiot,

Could you please tell me who the hell you are?

And if you are so-called myself, then I have only one

thing to say, "*Dear myself! Behave yourself.*"

Yours Untruly,
YOU

<>

"Is it the same mail that you sent to yourself?" Asked Nia.

Youvik sighed and nodded. He whispered. "Yes. I remember I sent it to myself approx a decade back. But how is this possible?"

Revik peered at the screen. "See the timestamp on the mail. The difference between the delivery time of both the mails is just a fraction of a second."

Youvik looked at him. "Does it mean that if my younger self replies to the mail from the future self in a split second, then my younger self can talk to my future self?"

"Possibly." Revik knelt. "But for that, your younger self needs to know that it's you, the future self, that is trying to reach out to him. And that he needs to reply within a fraction of a second."

Youvik took a deep breath. "I think that's what Ma had cracked and hence got a confirmation message from her younger self."

Revik looked at his grandmother's photo on the wall. "*Dadi,* you were a genius."

"I used to think..." Youvik added, "....that Ma was e-mailing me to make me improve my habits. When I asked her about it, she said the system had some virus and that even she'd get such silly mails."

Nia nodded. "I remember; during my college days, she had once asked to use our computer because she thought her's was glitching."

"Logically speaking," Revik pitched in. "Time travel is possible at only one location."

"Where is that?" Youvik was surprised.

"Geographic South Pole."

"Ah. That way. I know, intersecting point for all time zones."

"My baby is a genius," Nia caressed Revik's hair.

<>

The next day, Nia was ready to leave for work.

"Listen," said Youvik giving her the lunch box. "Take care and have a nice day."

"You better take care and stay away from that email." She said as she scratched the curry stain from his robe.

"I am utilizing my break from the corporate world not to rest but to spend some time with Revik."

"I am proud of you." She kissed his forehead. "Jenny was right. I have got the best husband."

"That reminds me." Youvik looked at a corner of the home."Revik and I have to decorate the temple for *Diwali*."

"That reminds me." She hugged him. "Happy *Dushehra*."

"Same to you, honey." He caressed her hair. "Call me after the session."

"Sure."

"By the way." He opened the door for her. "What's the topic for today's training?"

"Anger management."

<>

"Don't kill, but conquer the Ravana in you." Nia said, looking at the audience.

A lady from the audience raised her hand.

"Yes, please?"

"Sorry, Darling, I am afraid I don't know what *Ravana* is." She quipped.

"It's a character from the Holy book *Ramayana,* of Indian *Hindu* scriptures. Ravana represents the evil or anger or bad thoughts, and Lord Ram who killed him represents calmness or say good thoughts."

A person raised his hand. "And the historical day when Lord Rama killed Ravana, celebrated as Dushehra, is today."

"Right," Nia nodded. "That's why I used this quote to explain."

<>

"How was your day?" Nia asked, arranging the dinner table.

"Good. We researched a bit more on *mail-loop.*" Revik filling the water bottles.

"What is that?" She asked.

"Salt, please," Neel asked. He sprinkled some salt and pepper on his salad.

"Where is Daddy?" Nia asked Revik. He shrugged.

Youvik walked to the dinner table, and Nia smiled, seeing him in a white t-shirt and black Bermuda pants.

Neel smiled, looking at him, and prompted, "*Black and white, severally incomplete and at the same time completely several.*"

"Nice one, Dad," Youvik smiled. "You still remember the quotes."

"Mom," Revik closed the refrigerator. "Before you forget, a mail-loop is a situation when a mail from the future self gets stuck in a time-loop."

"Giving me a sense of *Deja Bhoo,*" said Youvik.

"By the way, Dad, I'm sorry," said Revik, pouring the soup. "The mail I had sent yesterday... I put my name in the signature as *Rev.*"

"Sorry?" Youvik asked, astonished.

"Sorry, Dad," he curled his lips. "It was just for fun."

"One second," he shut his eyes tight.

"Sorry, Daddy." Revik apologized.

Nia looked at him. "Why did you do that?"

"One second. I got your mail that day." Youvik came out of his reveries. "I got it the day Mom left us. I remember it now. It was signed by Revik."

"Seriously?" Revik was stunned.

"Yes," Youvik looked at him. "I clearly remember the day Mom left us. I had gotten a mail. The same one that we sent to me yesterday.

"That's a perfect example of a mail-loop," Revik smiled.

"I'll have to drill down further," said Youvik. He got up and stepped towards the study room. Revik followed suit.

"Guys," said Nia. "No one will leave without having dinner."

Revik looked at Youvik and came back to the table. Youvik did the same.

Neel was slurping the soup. Youvik slurped it in the same tone. He looked at him and he smiled back.

"Dad," said Youvik. "Story?"

Neel smiled and wiped his mouth with a napkin. "Which one?"

"Lord *Shiva* and the villagers."

Neel started narrating the story. He often forgot the story and characters in between, but Revik and Youvik helped him complete the story.

**

27.

Joy

Light up the lamps of...

◈

Light up the lamps of joy;
let there be smiles.

--

"We are getting late for *Diwali Pooja,*" said Nia rushing to the *Pooja* Room. "Youvik! Ask them if they are on their way."

A few moments, Youvik and his family were in the Pooja Room with Sam, Jenny, and their other friends. They chanted hymns and performed the *Aarti.* They were all seated on the floor except Neel and Jenny, who sat on the sofa.

Jenny's baby bump was very much visible.

After the *Pooja,* they exchanged hugs and gifts.

At the dining table, they exchanged loads of laughter.

"So, have you guys thought of a name for the princess?"

"Joy," said Sam, looking at Jenny.

Nia, Youvik, and Revik looked at each other in astonishment.

Sam looked at Jenny, "She thought of this name the day we got the results of the NIPT."

"What is NIPT?" Quipped Neel.

"Something similar to *peda* test in India." Youvik chuckled.

"I know *peda* is made from wheat flour, but this is the first time I hear of a *peda* test." Revik chuckled. "Anyways, a nice surprise for *Diwali*."

"Yeah," Jenny nodded. "But there are certain complications. Let's hope everything goes well."

"What's that?" Revik asked.

"Nothing, champ," Sam patted his back. "Anyway, do you know why we celebrate *Diwali* and so many other festivals?"

"Diwali is not just a festival of external lights, but it's also about illuminating the inner-self with lights of consciousness." He replied.

"He is a scholar." Sam patted him.

"The tagline is..." Revik added, *"Light up the lamps of joy; let there be smiles."*

"Well done, boy," Jenny bent forward to pat his back.

At that moment, she lost balance and slipped from the chair. Sam ran to hold her, but it was too late.

She fell to the floor and began to scream in extreme pain.

Youvik quickly dialled for an ambulance. They all rushed to the hospital.

<>

"I hope everything is okay," Nia told Youvik. They were in the hospital lobby. Sam was with the doctors.

"Hope so." Youvik consoled her.

"I think God is going to gift us, Joy," Revik said to give hope to everyone.

Youvik and Nia looked at him.

Revik held Nia's hand. "According to the mail, Joy was the daughter of Jenny."

"Yeah," Youvik was stunned to see his kid's composure and wit. "Let's hope for the best, and will Joy be safe?"

"I am sure she is safe," Revik said confidently. "That's what the e-mail from the future confirmed. Events can change, but the existence of people is certain."

"True that."

"Maybe in the future I am born to Mom, but my father is someone else."

He looked at Nia.

"I would still name you with R," smiled Nia. "The letter your *Nanu's* name starts with."

That moment, Sam came out smiling. "Joy is here. She looks like a little cute version of Jenny."

"Thank God!" Youvik got up, and Sam sobbed and hugged him.

"How is Jenny?" Nia asked as she consoled him.

"She had heavy bleeding. But it's all under control now."

**

28.

YOU

Build yourself...

◈

Build yourself,
You By You.

--

<>

15 years later

<>

Revik got out of his car and opened the door for his fiancé.

Nia greeted them as they made their way in.

"It's so good to see you finally." She chirped.

"Welcome to the family." Youvik hugged him and beamed at Revik. "Lucky chap."

Joy, who was standing on Revik's left, smiled. "I am his best man."

Revik smiled. He looked at Joy and then to his right. "Welcome home, Rio."

Rio looked at him. The couple smiled at each other lovingly. They were looking dashing in their turquoise suits.

Nia, along with Youvik, Joy, and her parents, welcomed the newlywed couple.

As Rio walked in, his eyes wandered over the passageway. "Mesmerising! I am taken by the way you have decorated your home. It doesn't seem like we're in London."

Revik cheered, "Now you know why this place was always a priority for my Cambridge getaway."

"No wonder," said Rio as he gaped at the assortment of trophies on the wall.

"I know your father is a researcher..." Rio added, but before he could complete the sentence, Revik interrupted him. "Our father."

"Oh, I am so sorry. My bad. So, I know our father is a researcher, but you never told me he is this talented!"

"Read it carefully," whispered Revik.

Noticing that Rio was a little hesitant, Youvik giggled. "Go on."

Rio moved closer, reading the labels, 'THE VOICE OF THE YOUTH,' 'THE NURTURER OF YOUNG MINDS,' 'ASK-ME-ANYTHING.'

He looked at Nia in awe and turned to Revik, "Amazing"

"My *Bro*, you know."

"Our *Bro*," Rio corrected him, and all laughed.

"Actually, I didn't want to boast that I have a great mom." Revik smiled.

"It's worth boasting, you dunce."

Nia smiled, "Well, it's all because of you, Revik."

"Come on, Ma, Don't be so humble," Revik nudged her.

"Call me *Bro* only, I like it that way only."

"Ok *Bro*, don't be so humble."

"No. I believed that a person could achieve something only during their youth. But when you started reading my first book... and showed appreciation... I realized that I could go on." Nia caressed Revik's chin.

"All your words are like pearls of wisdom. Maybe Rio will be your next fan," Revik looked at Rio.

"I already am," smiled Rio.

<>

They were all seated at the dining table. Nia served Rio some *Halwa*.

"Oh, no, no, no, no," said Rio. "Not too much, please. I am on a strict no-sugar diet for our wedding."

"Don't worry," Revik chuckled. "Mom won't allow me to dump you even if you cross your BMI."

"It's made with *jaggery*," Nia told Rio. "Good sugar, you know."

"So Revik," Youvik said. He picked up a spoon. "How is your new project working out? Did you find an investor?"

"Dad," he smiled. He pulled the spoon from Youvik's hand. "This good sugar is no good for you anymore."

"I..." Youvik mumbled. He looked at Nia. "I was about to give it to you my boy."

"Better. Anyway, you know how the corporate world is. I found one guy. He is the best in terms of understanding my vision. But he's a bit sceptical right now," he continued. "I have given him five detailed presentations. I don't know how else to convince him."

"Stretch yourself; be or do, different." Nia advised him. "Just tell them their issues, and then show how your solution is one-size-fits-all."

"Ma. If it didn't work out five times, it's not going to work the sixth time." Revik prompted.

"With the touch of wisdom, comes the end of fears." Youvik added, relishing his almonds.

"Wow, Dad," Revik slow clapped. "This is the first time I hear something like this from you."

"It's from your Mommy's book."

"That's why," Revik chuckled. "Anyway, I am working on our project too; religiously. Just this one thing sets me back by ten steps each time."

"Oh!" Youvik's eyes widened. "I didn't think you would find time for it. What is it? Maybe I could help."

"It's the timeline problem. It makes me lose faith. How can we prove or disprove it?"

"By sending a mail to yourself in the past, simple," Youvik beamed.

"Yes. But if we have no read receipts and no changes in the current timeline, we can't prove it in our time."

"Then maybe you'll have to ask your younger-self to send you a confirmation mail."

Revik snapped his brows, "That's a good idea. I can request a reply."

"Or," Youvik snapped his fingers. "A read-mail-request program that will attach itself to the mail."

"Mind-bending, thought-provoking." Revik got up to

kiss Youvik.

"Life, multi-faceted life; roles, multi-hatted; pick and play, at your best." Nia smiled.

"From your next book Ma?" Revik taking a sip of coffee, "Sorry *Bro*. By the way what's the title of your next book?"

She looked at Youvik, "YOU."

"I need good share of your royalties," Youvik winked, "By the way what's the tag line?"

"Build yourself, You By You." She smiled, "Inspired by you."

"That's cool..." Revik looked at Rio.

"Indeed," said Rio finishing finished the last bit of Halwa. "I don't know what exactly you guys are talking about, but I want to go in the past and apologize to Mom for asking her not to serve this Halwa."

"You are welcome."

"Oops, sorry. Thank you for this mind-bending Halwa, and it gives me a thought-provoking craving," Rio said, extending the empty bowl. "Just a bowl full. Could I, please."

All laughed as Nia served him.

<>

The next morning Revik and Rio were in the kitchen preparing breakfast.

"Breakfasts are made in heaven; couples, in the kitchen."

Laughed Nia as Youvik followed her to the balcony.

They all settled on the balcony on their sun-basking chairs. Sam, Jenny, and Joy joined them.

"Guys!" Revik called out. "Breakfast was my duty today. So, here is Dad's favourite beaten coffee and Mom's favourite bandaged sandwiches."

"White t-shirt and black Bermuda?" Nia asked Revik. "Didn't you buy this just last week? To wear at home?"

"Black and white, as if generations relived; over and again," winked Revik.

Youvik looked at him, smiling, "Your *Dadu* must be proud. I'm sure he's watching over you from heaven above through his telescope."

That moment Youvik's mobile chimed. Youvik was shocked to see that it was a mail from his own ID. Everyone was busy chatting, but Revik was observing him, "All well, Dad?"

He gave him the mobile. The message read -

<>

Dear YOU,

I am not sure if this mail will reach you, but I am so glad that Joy is marrying Ritik. I never imagined that my son-in-law would be none other than the son of the girl my Mom had once selected for me.

I am attaching their photos and the wedding card below. Please do visit if you happen to invent the time-travel in the parallel universe ;)

Yours truly,
YOU

<>

"I don't understand, Dad," Revik looked at Youvik. "And could it be that Revik is misspelled as Ritik?"

"The name is correct. Nia always said she'd name her child with an 'R.' Anyway, look at the attachment."

Revik was astonished to see the wedding photo of the couple. Ritik almost resembled him.

Then he quickly scrolled down to read the wedding card, and mother-in-law was none other than Nia.

"See, I told you," Revik was excited. "Life repeats. Story is same; people change."

Nia looked at them and guessed what they were discussing.

Later they filled her in. Nia was astonished to see the wedding photo.

<>

At noon, they all settled for lunch. Their gossips were unending.

"Where are you guys headed for tomorrow?" Rio asked, sipping coffee.

Nia looked at Youvik. "The place we missed while your dad was posted in London for the first time."

"O God," exclaimed Revik. "You are still after him for not taking you to that place?"

Youvik chuckled. "She won't let me die until I take her there."

She threw the newspaper at him. "Crap."

He picked up the newspaper and looked at the advertisement, "I'm gonna by these winter gears for our next trip."

***

About the Author

Vikrmn is the pen name of CA Vikram Verma who has authored many books so far. Along with being a Chartered Accountant and a decade and a half in Banking Regulatory & Risk Compliance, his dexterity bags creative pursuits of artwork and poetry.

10 Golden Steps of Life, Guru with Guitar and 10 Alone are his motivational novels that are cited globally for life-changing quotes. *Agile Able, LIBOR Plan B and MICS Unleashed* are his books for professionals. The author is reachable at **www.vikrmn.com**.

www.ingramcontent.com/pod-product-compliance
Lightning Source LLC
LaVergne TN
LVHW090321210926
848480LV00001B/322
* 9 7 9 8 8 8 8 8 3 3 0 0 1 *